OUSMANE
SEMBÈNE

Indiana University Press · Bloomington and Indianapolis

OUSMANE SEMBÈNE

THE MAKING OF A MILITANT ARTIST

Samba Gadjigo

Translated by Moustapha Diop · With a Foreword by Danny Glover

This book is a publication of

Indiana University Press
601 North Morton Street
Bloomington, IN 47404-3797 USA

www.iupress.indiana.edu

Telephone orders	800-842-6796
Fax orders	812-855-7931
Orders by e-mail	iuporder@indiana.edu

Originally published as _Ousmane Sembène: Une conscience africaine,_
© 2007 Homnisphères
© 2010 Indiana University Press
All rights reserved

∞ The paper used in this publication meets the minimum requirements
of the American National Standard for Information Sciences—Permanence
of Paper for Printed Library Materials, ANSI Z39.48-1992.

Manufactured in the United States of America

Library of Congress Cataloging-in-Publication Data

Gadjigo, Samba, [date]
  [Ousmane Sembène. English]
  Ousmane Sembène : the making of a militant artist / Samba Gadjigo ;
translated by Moustapha Diop ; foreword by Danny Glover.
      p. cm.
  Translation of: Ousmane Sembène : une conscience africaine :
genèse d'un destin hors du commun. Paris : Homnisphères, c2007.
  Includes bibliographical references and index.
  ISBN 978-0-253-35413-6 (cloth : alk. paper) — ISBN 978-0-253-22151-3 (pbk. :
alk. paper) 1. Sembène, Ousmane, 1923–2007. 2. Sembène, Ousmane, 1923–2007
—Political and social views. 3. Authors, Senegalese—20th century—Biography.
4. Motion picture producers and directors—Senegal—Biography. 5. Senegalese
literature (French)—History and criticism. 6. Senegal—Intellectual life. 7. Senegal
—Colonial influence. 8. Postcolonialism—Social aspects—Senegal. 9. Casamance
(Senegal)—Biography. 10. Marseille (France)—Biography. I. Title.
  PQ3989.S46Z6613 2010
  843'.914—dc22
  [B]
                              2009037116

1 2 3 4 5 15 14 13 12 11 10

Frontispiece: Ousmane Sembène.
Courtesy of Thomas Jacob.

*To Cheikh Anta Diop, Nelson Mandela, and
all those who devote their life and work to the
political and cultural unification of Africa*

Dawn was breaking—dawn, the fight between night and day. But the night was exhausted and could fight no more, and slowly died. A few rays of the sun, the forerunners of this victory of the day, still hovered on the horizon, pale and timid, while the last stars gently glided under the mass of clouds, crimson like the blooming flamboyant flowers.

Keïta Fodeba, Aube africaine, quoted in Frantz Fanon,
The Wretched of the Earth, trans. Constance Farrington
(New York: Grove Press, 1963), 228

Overleaf: Ousmane Sembène.
Courtesy of Ousmane Sembène.

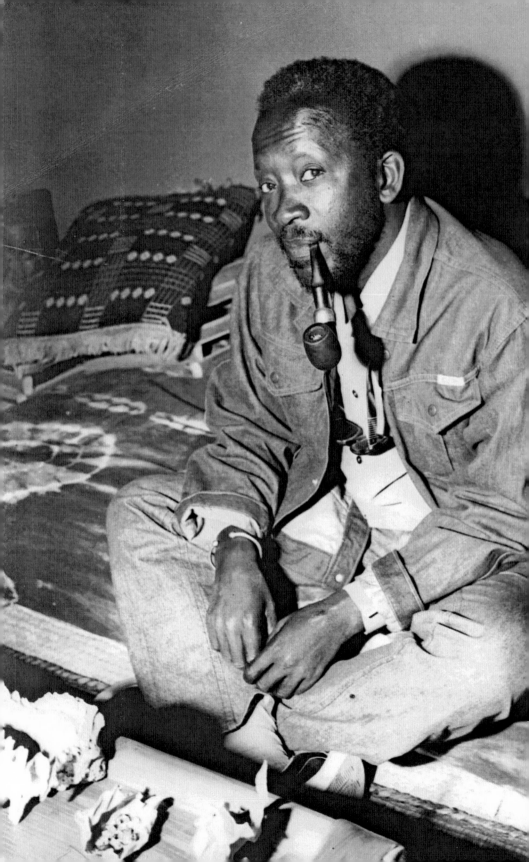

CONTENTS

FOREWORD

Danny Glover

Ousmane Sembène was one of the world's most passionate filmmakers, and the novelist who perhaps best captured the turmoil of modern West Africa. He was a staunchly political figure who, in an era of violent power plays, used storytelling as a means of leverage. He was a visionary who understood the power of imagination as a form of resistance against the colonizer, and as a means of cultivating awareness, integrity, and compassion for a better future. He was a leader who helped create a filmmaking labor union, a film festival, and a literary magazine. He was, in sum, one of Africa's most important cultural figures of the twentieth century. And to me, he was both a hero and a friend.

I remember when I first saw *Black Girl* (*La Noire de . . .*) in the 1960s, when I was a student and at the same time reading Frantz Fanon's *Wretched of the Earth*. That mask! The way Sembène's ever-observant yet mysteriously unobtrusive camera captured the slow emptying of soul that was Diouana's death. Our relationship began there, though he couldn't know that until we actually met in August of 1988 at his home in Dakar. I had come specifically to Senegal to meet Sembène. I remember him serving the Senegalese dish called *yassa* over a grain that was grown precolonialism called *funio,* and explaining the origins of the grain. So in that small way Sembène was teaching, giving voice to the past and history.

Yes, Sembène was an African storyteller, but it wasn't the color of his characters' skin that resonated with me (though it remains true, nearly 50 years after Sembène first picked up a camera, that those of us with dark skin are still fighting to overcome racism in the global movie-making system). Sembène's movies were not solely about race. He told the stories neglected by the international media, stories of people living and loving, through tragedy and triumph, on the margins of society. More consistently than any artist I know, Sembène gave voice and agency to everyday people coping with and battling against everyday injustices—allowing us to anoint our own heroes and simultaneously revealing the mechanics of the systems responsible for those injustices. Systems that encourage cruelty, not compassion, and narrow-mindedness instead of imagination. Sembène's films and novels suggest a better way. He didn't lecture us, and didn't rant. Instead, he gave us beautiful, eloquent, moving stories, rich with metaphor and image. My own efforts as an actor, producer, and filmmaker are inspired by his—and our bond of friendship and artistic understanding culminated in 2007 when he and his family entrusted me with and granted me the rights to produce a screen adaptation of his magisterial novel *God's Bits of Wood.*

All of Sembène's ten novels have been translated into several languages. His films have been seen around the world. It isn't their African-ness that appeals to so many people. His are not the typically shallow stories and images that the Western media give us of Africa. There is not a white hero adventurer, an elephant or lion, or a bloated child covered with flies to be seen in Sembène's work. He used stories to connect us—the global masses—together. These are universal stories that would be, I imagine, as relevant to an Indian farmer as to a Senegalese secretary, to a dockworker in Brooklyn as to a sheepherder in Ukraine.

Sadly, but not at all surprisingly, Sembène's works remained largely unseen and unread by those they were intended for. Especially in Africa, the movies remain hard to find, and, when not openly obstructed by various government authorities, have never been given their proper distribution. Sembène died in 2007, just three years after his last artistic triumph, *Moolaade,* which I had the privilege to help finance, and which won awards around the world. Yet even that film remains unknown to most people in Senegal and West Africa. It falls to all of us now to resurrect the great cultural workers and heroes of Africa, and especially for Africa's people and its vast diaspora.

Samba Gadjigo is carrying Sembène's torch forward, with this, the first part of a two-volume biography. This is a work that reflects both a high level of scholarship, and the deep commitment to African progress that Sembène embodied. Dr. Gadjigo has dedicated much of the past 15 years to understanding Sembène, his works and their contexts, and this book thus informs not just about an artist, but of a place and time. I hope this biography inspires other researchers, activists, and artists to study Sembène, and to create work that honors his substantial, essential legacy.

PREFACE

In 1972, I was in my senior year at the Faidherbe High School in Saint-Louis, the first capital of French West Africa (AOF). The educational institution, today known as the Omar Tall High School, was named after Louis-Léon César Faidherbe, the famous polytechnician and civil engineering officer who was appointed governor of Senegal in 1852. This was France's first significant educational achievement in Black Africa, and one of the "jewels" of the colonial education system—although such a glorious past is quite at odds with the current rundown state of the building. One could name, among the school's alumni, Alioune Diop, the great cultural worker, founder of *Présence Africaine;* the writer Birago Diop; Dr. Jacques Diouf, director-general of the Food and Agriculture Organization of the United Nations (FAO); and the artist-painter Iba Ndiaye.

In the '70s, the teaching staff at Faidherbe High School consisted mainly of French "development workers." Our curriculum was still drawing, especially in literature, upon the fabled textbook *Lagarde et Michard.*[1] We could easily recite from memory Molière, Racine, Baudelaire, and other "monuments" of French literature. But what about African writers? According to the above-named textbook writers, they simply did not exist. In other words, there was nothing worth reading coming from the colonies. Now, colonialism is essentially a system of oppression, and as such it is bound— or doomed—to constantly carry within itself the seeds of its own undoing. Thus, sometimes it comes to pass that a casual, seemingly insignificant event triggers the salutary awakening process in the mind of colonized or neo-colonized peoples. The arrival in our high school of a new French literature teacher in 1972 was such an "unlikely" catalyst.

France was still reeling from the May '68 student demonstrations. The old Republic, which until then had been thought to be standing on firm ground, was nearly swept away, along with its institutions, in a tidal wave of insurrectional activities, tire-burning, tear gases, showdowns at the barricades with the police, and surrealist slogans inspired by Arthur Rimbaud, the *enfant terrible* of French literature.[2] De Gaulle was, however, quick to regain control of the situation. Then followed a secret witch-hunt, as reaction sought to weed out or ostracize radical academics. Thus came from Nanterre, hotbed of these anti-establishment firebrands, one Mrs. Pagot. At the time, we hardly suspected that she had been sent to Africa as one would send an unruly teenager to a youth correctional facility: this "exile" in Africa was supposed to cool her revolutionary fervor and wean her away from radical politics—but this disciplinary measure would be to no avail. Our superintendent entrusted Mrs. Pagot with the senior classes, including ours. For the first time in our life we had to study, as part of the curriculum, Frantz Fanon's *The Wretched of the Earth*[3] and . . . Ousmane Sembène's *God's Bits of Wood*.[4]

Sembène was born in Casamance, in the southern region of Senegal. Before gaining prominence as a writer and filmmaker, he worked as a docker in the Marseilles harbor. I felt there was magic at work in this course of life, which struck me as that of a legendary figure, outsmarting Fate and beating it at its own game. You could hear a pin drop during Mrs. Pagot's class, as a studious silence hung over a room usually astir with the voices of boisterous teenagers. For one whole month we studied Sembène's work really hard. Dakar, Thiès, Bamako, Saint-Louis: in the novel we kept coming across the names of cities that sounded so familiar to us. Some of us even bore the same name as characters in *God's Bits of Wood,* and soon my classmates were to dub me Samba Ndoulougou, one of the most colorful characters in the novel.

To say that we could directly relate to a work so steeped in our actual world "out there," is to repeat the obvious. We were in our late teens, at that crossroads between adolescence and adulthood, and Sembène was telling us about colonization, Blacks and whites, and the need to push for change. He quickly became our idol. To us, classes with Mrs. Pagot meant no longer attending literature classes, only to hear some Apollinaire poeticize about the Pont Mirabeau; instead, it was like standing at a window that looked out onto our real life. Through this mere novel, we caught a glimpse into a world—actually *ours*—which proved to be an intricate fabric woven out of juvenile, sometimes a bit wild, dreams, and an ever-present angst.

Sembène was rarely mentioned in classes during my undergraduate years at the University of Dakar; and when such was the case, it was then only in passing. All the same, I felt drawn to the study of African literature, and my mentor, Prof. Madior Diouf, encouraged me to fulfill my newfound calling. Yet many years would elapse before I had, at last, an opportunity to meet Sembène himself, in flesh and blood. The meeting took place in 1989, on the premises of his production company, Filmii Doomireew, which was then located at 36, Rue Abdoukarim Bourgi, in Dakar.

I was at that time a junior lecturer at Mount Holyoke College, in Massachusetts. I had just come to hand Sembène an invitation from the Five College African Studies Council for a one-month visit during an event organized in the Pioneer Valley. That long-anticipated first meeting was a total failure, to say the least; it certainly did not match my expectations. On that day, Sembène struck me as particularly boorish, and I sensed a slight note of hostility in his gruff voice. "Why do you want to invite me? Don't you have my works? So just study them, and forget about the rest." He did not seem to have any time for a bothersome young academic like me. I was actually on the verge of tears, but my stubbornness somehow managed to get the better of him. "Alright, give me the invitation," he mumbled. "I'll think about it, ok?" I realized our meeting had come to an end. In March 1990, Sembène *did* make the trip to the United States. For two weeks (instead of the envisioned four) he took part in discussions of his work and gave lectures in many African Studies classes, to the great delight of both faculty and students. It was a resounding success, but Sembène the artist restricted his answers and comments to the contents of his works. As usual, he remained secretive about "the man Sembène."

Ousmane Sembène is, without any doubt, to be counted among the most productive contemporary African artists, in terms of both literary and cinematic output. No African Studies program worthy of the name can ignore him. His movies have earned him awards and prizes at all the great film events on the five continents. He gave a "movie lesson" at the 2005 Cannes Festival, a rare mark of respect shown to prominent film directors for their experience and creativity. As befits a man of his stature, literary and film critics have devoted numerous scholarly articles to his work, and scores of M.A. and Ph.D. dissertations deal extensively with either or both aspects of his artistic output, filmmaking and writing.

However, in spite of a rich artistic career spanning nearly half a century, Ousmane Sembène remains something of an unknown celebrity. One is indeed hard put to name any single study devoted to the life experiences out of which Sembène's work grew and took shape. The late Paulin Soumanou Vieyra, his friend and erstwhile assistant, made a first attempt at cutting through the thick mist that surrounds Sembène's life like a protective halo.[5] His groundbreaking monograph is of great significance for the study of Sembène's films, but Vieyra provides little insight into Sembène's life and tribulations. In fact, fewer than 25 pages are devoted to "the man Sembène," in an eponymous chapter.

The main goal of the present book is ultimately to bridge this gap. Moreover, I regard this task as a sort of *minding* work, a "duty of memory" in reaction to our nearly criminal tendency to indulge in amnesia and to cast into oblivion whole chunks of our history. More often than not, we do not know anything about the valiant men and women who gave their life so that our peoples may live in freedom and dignity. On the other hand, everywhere on the African continent we jealously preserve the monuments built in honor of the foreign "heroes" who were actually our most bloodthirsty oppressors. Can there be a more humiliating paradox? Do we not celebrate April 4th, Independence Day in Senegal, on the Boulevard du Général de Gaulle?

Thus, far from being a mere piece of routine scholarly work, the present biography, while uncompromisingly based on the principles of historical research, does not shy away from political issues. My intention is also to cast in sharper relief the life of a man whose discordant, countervailing voice the establishment discourse in Senegal, political and/or religious, is keen on containing within "proper" bounds. Furthermore, even though I have made it a point to scrupulously comply with some rules of biographical research, it quickly became clear to me that within the African context, more than anywhere else, the researcher is hampered by a lack of written sources and archives. However, this chronic paucity did not deter me from proceeding with my research. The following "reconstruction" consists of the testimonies of men and women who knew Sembène during his youth and his formative years. I am greatly indebted to those who helped me, as we have laid the foundation for future research, for others to probe deeper into Sembène's life.

The present biography is divided into four sections that follow, chronologically, Sembène's life, from his birth in 1923 to 1956, the year that his first literary work, *Black Docker,* was published. In spite of the above-mentioned impediments, I have tried to provide, at every stage, insight into the various experiences he has been through and the influences that were to prove crucial to his way of perceiving the world and of living in it. In the process, I also quickly came to realize that this type of research could represent a tough challenge, given my personal itinerary.

Let it be clearly stated, however, that the door to Sembène's study, in Yoff, was wide open for me; he had granted me full-time access, even during his absence. It was a fruitful, instructive, and at times moving experience: there I found traces of his readings and could relive the atmosphere in which he liked to work, and I also leafed through numerous scholarly monographs on his work. The house became for me a living document, a goldmine of information—mapped out by a welter of clues, easily detectable or almost invisible—on the artist, the larger-than-life man. However, for all these rewarding experiences, I still sensed an ever-present void, something akin to that enigmatic and sobering silence amid the sound and fury of our lives. When one has been teaching in the United States for nearly two decades, one is easily unsettled and frustrated by the lack of written correspondence and documentation; it was hard for me to come to terms with the fact that almost no data on Sembène's life was available. Sometimes, the person one is writing a biography on can help overcome these hurdles. Unfortunately, Sembène seldom talks about himself. "The work I have done is what matters most. As to my poor self, I want to remain anonymous, lost among the crowd." Many episodes of his life are still clouded in mystery, and in such cases his kinfolk and circle of friends are often of little help. Nevertheless, these hindrances have led me to cast aside some preconceived notions about proper academic research: today I know from firsthand experience that a good "reconstruction" can make up for a lack or insufficiency of written documents. The point is less about denying the paramount importance of written sources than about relativizing their role. Storytelling and the recollections of eyewitnesses have often served as a means of conveying the experiences stored in individual and collective memories. Besides, the verb "to tell" already implies the notion of verbal performance. I have been "in the field" and met the people who have been part of Sembène's life, painstakingly recording their accounts. A carefully conducted library research has enabled me to recreate the settings and context of his life. As Ahmadou Hampathé Bâ's famous dictum has it: "In Africa the death of an old man is like the burning of a library." Yet one cannot stop death from taking its toll of human lives, and few of those who knew Ousmane Sembène during his childhood, his youth, and his "Marseilles years" are still alive. I had thus to act quickly and speak with these old acquaintances before it was too late. To put it briefly, the challenges were both overwhelming and exciting. I could have come up with a more voluminous output, but as I said earlier, this is only a modest contribution to a fight against forgetfulness that should be regarded as a collective undertaking. With regard to Ousmane Sembène's life, at the very least, I have made it a point to pave the way for future generations of researchers, so that they shall not be condemned to perpetually start from scratch.

Part 1, "On the Banks of a Mighty River: Ousmane Sembène's Childhood," highlights the complexity of Sembène's family background. As the son of a Lebu (Master of the Waters) who was also a Muslim and had migrated to the Joola country, the lush natural scenery imbued Sembène with a deep sense of wonder; the diversity of languages and religions, so typical of the social environment in Casamance, along with the cult of moral integrity and free thinking, the basic traits shared by all the ethnic groups of Casamance, would be influential in the shaping of his artistic individuality. The period covers the years 1923–1938, right before he "definitively" leaves Casamance to settle in Dakar. This first section places great emphasis on the values upon which Sembène drew to form his personal ethics and on the tensions he had to internalize and manage at an early age.

Part 2, "Dakar: The Turbulent Years," documents the years 1938–1944, before his departure for war. In the natives' shantytowns of the Dakar Plateau, which Birago Diop vividly portrays in *La plume raboutée*,[6] the young Sembène discovers his Lebu heritage: the sea, the sun, wanderlust and, more importantly, a rich and multifaceted cultural life. These Dakar years are also marked by two pivotal moments: his entry into the world of labor and his first contacts with literature and cinema. Surrounded and constantly pushed back toward the periphery as the European city grew, the Lebu community of Dakar bitterly experienced colonial marginality and otherness. The young Sembène could not feel unconcerned about daily injustices, primarily within his own group as well as in their interactions with colonial authorities.

Within the framework of this study, one point of reference will be the bombing of Dakar by the Allied Forces on September 25, 1940. At stake behind this military operation was the conquest of Dakar, then still controlled by the Vichy administration. The native population that bore the brunt of the attack had no idea why they were thus hurled into the dark days of food rationing, economic stagnation, deprivation, and violence. For a while Sembène eagerly sought refuge in religion, before he enrolled in the army.

February 1st marks another watershed: at the age of 21, Sembène enlists in the army. I have devoted most of part 3 to this army experience, which Sembène describes, not without a whiff of self-dramatization, as the "greatest school" of his life. "The war taught me everything," he readily declares. For nearly two years he would be stationed in the Niger desert as a private in the Transportation Unit. Interestingly enough, for all the bullying, the humiliations, and the segregation, Sembène fought alongside his French comrades with a deeply felt love for the "fatherland." Like every colonial of his generation, the would-be anticolonialist writer was sincerely ready to die for France. The rest of this strange love affair is well-known: when Africans later decided to fight for their own freedom, France did not hesitate to machine-gun them down wholesale, as was the case in Thiaroye, Senegal, in 1944 and in Sétif, Algeria, in 1945. These various experiences would eventually lead to Sembène's rude awakening from the slumber of colonial subservience. His break with religion is the first indication of this heightened self-consciousness.

In 1946, after the war, Sembène was back in Dakar, where a new wind was blowing over the country. Faced with economic recession, the workers, ideology-wiser and better organized, stepped up their demands. To their plea for social justice the colonial administration responded with mere political trickery and deceits. Part 4 goes straight to the core of Sembène's commitment. Here the future author of *God's Bits of Wood* comes to grips with the struggle of trade unions and the "categorical imperative" of challenging a debilitating status quo. Additionally, he meets for the very first time in his life the men and women whose influence would eventually leave an enduring stamp on his work. But for Sembène this period was mainly synonymous with discontent and a diffuse, still unfocused feeling of spite toward colonialism, the climax of a dramatic quest that would subsequently lead him to Marseilles, in France.

Sembène's itinerary between 1947 and 1956 is a critical period in his artistic and militant training. Indeed, in his case it is hard to draw a line between art and activism. At every point in his life both have fed on and strengthened each other. When he became a docker in the Marseilles harbor, new vistas and possibilities opened up. He interacted every day with other African migrants and experienced like them the full force of exploitation and racism; like them, he also lived in a narrow, closed environment. At the time, he was keenly interested in learning all about communist, internationalist, and openly anticolonialist ideologies, leftist movements and, on a more concrete level, organized action. His revolutionary culture was acquired through diligent readings. In the heat of union and political struggles, his political consciousness became more assertive and he discovered a new calling: the fight for Africa as a whole.

The young Sembène arrives in Marseilles fully determined to make up for lost time. His poor school training, far from being a handicap, makes him all the more eager to learn. He divides his time between work, union activity, and reading in the libraries of the powerful General Confederation of Labor (CGT) and the French Communist Party (PCF). During his study time, he would encounter, through their works, writers and progressives from all over the world, such as Vercors (the pen name of Jean Bruller), Richard Wright, Nazim Hikmet, and Jacques Roumain, among many others.

However, in this chorus of generous voices, none rose from Africa to convey the thirst for freedom of the workers, farmers, and women of a continent that already seemed cut off from the rest of the world and living in a state of limbo. This painful realization impelled Sembène's foundational vision: the struggle for a better, more decent life or for political rights is doomed to fail if the cultural dimension is left out of the equation. His firm belief that "man is primarily a cultural animal" led to Sembène's involvement, starting in 1951, with literary groups and in youth hostels (a space for political exchange), and aroused his interest in "red dramatics," the forerunner of social protest theater. The more he attended poetry recitals and took part in writing workshops, the sharper his artistic sensibility grew. In part 4, "The Making of a Militant-Artist," I deal with the various stages of this artistic training, which can be said to have been nearly complete by 1956, with the publications of his first poem, "Liberté" (Freedom) in the review *La Croix du Sud* and of his novel *Le docker noir* by Editions Debresse.

I have deliberately elected to restrict the scope of this biography to Sembène's early youth and formative years. Research into other parts of his life will be conducted eventually, I truly hope, so as to highlight his contribution to the history of ideas and his lifelong involvement in the promotion of African culture.

ACKNOWLEDGMENTS

More than a duty, it is a pleasure for me to express my gratitude to all the individuals and institutions whose contribution made this work possible. Of course, special debt is owed to Mount Holyoke College, which provided, at many points in the research process, generous financial support to fund my numerous trips to Africa and Europe, as well as within the United States, to gather research material.

In Ziguinchor, Marie Dia, Ousmane Sembène's elder half-sister; Moussa Barro, a childhood friend; "Dimitri," his nephew; and Abbé Diamacoune Senghor are acknowledged for sharing with me, during long conversations, crucial information concerning Sembène's early years. My special thanks also to Maurice Ousseynou Fall, who provided most of the material I needed for the Dakar episodes. As a playmate during their teenage years, and one of Sembène's most trusted confidants until his death in 1998, Maurice Fall was throughout a valuable resource person. A generous, cultivated, and self-effacing former land registry officer, he recreated for me the old Lebu neighborhoods and settlements in Dakar, especially in the Plateau.

In Marseilles, longtime activists and comrades who Sembène fought alongside in the '50s helped me get a better grasp of the most salient features of his trade union experience and the various influences that shaped his political and artistic temperament. I am particularly indebted to the group of retirees from the Union of Dockers at La Joliette. Odette Arouh and Michel Libermann also deserve special acknowledgment for their insightful information on the leftist organizations and literary circles of which Sembène was a part in Marseilles.

In Paris, Med Hondo and the late Malagasy poet Jacques Rabemananjara have been tremendously helpful. Thanks are also due to my friends Lamine and Monique Konté, and Mamadou Sylla as well. Ousmane Sène, a professor at Cheikh Anta Diop University in Dakar, and Mody Guiro, who introduced me to the world of railroad workers in Thiès, provided knowledgeable information and detailed accounts that substantially advanced this project. I am immensely grateful to Boubacar Boris Diop for his intellectual insights and generous, painstaking reading and editing of the manuscript.

To my wife, Hotia, and my sons, Ali and Malik, thanks for your love and your patience.

Last but not least, special thanks to Ousmane Sembène, who obliged in ways too many to acknowledge here and gave me full access to his house, Gallè Ceddo, as a research base. In the course of this project, just his name opened many doors to us.

OUSMANE
SEMBÈNE

PART ONE

ON THE BANKS OF A MIGHTY RIVER

Ousmane Sembène's Childhood

Ousmane Sembène in front of his birthplace, his father's house in Ziguinchor, 1972. *Photo courtesy of Ousmane Sembène.*

*The pungent smell of flower-covered liana was inter-
spersed with lingering odors of hot oil and smoke.*

*The boat resumed its slow upstream course on the
river. The water was thick and yellowish; on one side of
the riverbed stretched the bulrush-coated plain, where
the caimans had their dwellings. One could also catch
a glimpse of the far edge of the bush, where a thousand
hazards lurked. Flocks of heavy-feathered birds flew
over the reeds, brushing them lightly with their wings;
marabouts dipped their beaks in the pond in search of
fish before soaring to dizzying heights. The boat was
drawing close to the right bank, where the bush-trees
swooped forward in a mad rush toward the river. The
front-row trees bent eagerly over the glaucous water,
their branches and lianas interwoven in a dazzling
chaos, a truly anarchic vegetal webwork. The palm-
trees lay supine on the river and offered their rugged
trunks for the young caimans to rest upon, as if they
were themselves tired of the corrosive water, of all this
wild bustle tossing them around; their palm fronds
rocked to the rhythm of the stream like floating algae.*

—Ousmane Sembène, *O pays, mon beau peuple!*

1

Casamance

Casamance, Sembène's native region, holds a prominent place in his imagination. This artistic investment in a locality pervades his entire corpus, from *O pays, mon beau peuple!* (1957) through *L'harmattan* (1963), a novel centered around the 1958 referendum organized by Charles de Gaulle, a momentous event purported to determine the future of French colonies in Africa; and to *Emitaï* (1971), Sembène's first historical movie, cast against a backdrop of war memories. Casamance is also the region from which hails Diouana, the tragic heroine of *Black Girl*, Sembène's 1962 short story about a Senegalese woman experiencing *petit-bourgeois* neo-slavery in France. Diouana, like thousands of lower-class girls and women in post-independence Dakar, is forced to haunt the sidewalks of residential areas in the hope that some "emancipated" French woman will hire her as a maid. In a passage strongly reminiscent of the slave markets of old, the "Black girl" is picked out of a crowd of mostly old native women by an uppity French lady. When she and her husband move back to France, they take Diouana along, entrusting her with the care of their children. But there, in the Côte d'Azur, Diouana realizes that her employers only want to suck the life out of her, and do not care at all about her personal background, her desires, or her plans for the future. In the end Diouana slits her veins open in the bathtub. Sembène later turned this tragic story into the movie *Black Girl,* an adaptation that is both unpretentious in its representational style and gripping in its emotional thrust.

But the word "Casamance" calls to mind, above all, the river that bears the same name, a river at once enthralling and mysterious, calm and restless, actor in and witness to a tumultuous history. When the Mandingo griots compose songs about Casamance, they celebrate an entire community. Casamance, Ousmane Sembène's "kingdom of childhood," is also the land dear to his fictional alter ego, Oumar Faye, the main character in *O pays, mon beau peuple!,* who returns home full of haunting dreams, after years of war, exile, and learning in Europe. Actually, it is the writer himself who returns to his native land. Sembène was born on the right bank of the river, called Lower Casamance, a region cluttered with marsh creeks, locally known as *bolongs.* These *bolongs* were Ousmane Sembène's favorite haunts during his childhood years. He once declared that the early period of his life can be summed up in four words: "swimming, fishing, tree-climbing and hunting."[1]

Casamance is located in the southern part of Senegal, between the Gambian enclave in the north and the Bissau-Guinean border in the south. The region has a surface area of 30,000 square kilometers and bears the name of the 156-mile-long river that cuts it in half. The climate is of the wet tropical type, with a rainy season and abundant vegetation. The lower river valley consists of a long and narrow estuary whose shores are lined with mangroves and palm trees, due to the oceanic upwelling off the Atlantic coast. In Lower Casamance, the Joolas, along with their subgroups (including Floups, Mandjaks, and Balantes), form the bulk of the population. In spite of the long-lasting effects of Christianization, traditional religion is still widely practiced. In the early twentieth century, as other parts of Senegal were being plagued with chronic drought, Wolofs, Muslims, and peanut growers flocked to the fertile lands of this region.

From the Atlantic, in the west, imagine you are following the upstream progress of a ship on the right bank: you soon reach Lower Casamance. After rounding the Karabane island, you come to Elinkine, the Soninke enclave, home of the legendary Djignabo Badji, who led an attack on the French military base of Séléki[2] and was executed on May 18, 1906, by the French troops for instigating a rebellion.[3] Toward the northwest and the refreshing but riotous waters of the Soungrougrou, one of its tributaries, the river curls up on itself and bends like a sickle at the Pointe Saint-Georges, before flowing away to the northeast and making a stop, as it were, at Ziguinchor.

This city, Casamance's administrative capital, is where Ousmane Sembène was born, deep in the heart of the former Kaabu empire, a region known for its unique fauna and flora. The prestige of the Kaabu people is something of a legend, and even today Mandingo griots like to sing paeans to the memory of their former kings, their *Mansas,* while playing on their koras. The kora, a musical instrument made up of 21 strings, is so intimately connected to the expression of self for the natives of Casamance that Ousmane Sembène himself did not hesitate to point out that for him "the kora is the ultimate symbol of the creative act; it has many strings: I play it as I please and I just want to get from it the most beautiful sounds."[4] Among the great kora players with whom this river country has blessed the world, the names Lamine Konté and Soundioulou Cissoko stand out most prominently. Lamine Konté put kora on the international cultural map and worked with scores of world-class artists, including Stevie Wonder in a collaboration for the soundtrack of Walon Green's 1978 *Journey through the Secret Life of Plants*—a documentary based on Stevie Wonder's eponymous album. Soundioulou Cissoko, who was Sembène's schoolmate, plucked the strings of his instrument on the highly popular national radio, casting his "good spell" through the airwaves for more than 30 years.

Ousmane Sembène spent the first 12 years of his life in Ziguinchor, totally immersed in its daily activities. Every now and then he would go to Marsassoum, in the northeast (Middle Casamance), to visit his great-uncle Abdourahmane Diop.

For Sembène, Casamance is the hotbed that quickened his creative genius. It is also the land he evokes in beautiful, poignant descriptions that are at times imbued with a tragic lyricism that is all his own, as in *O pays, mon beau peuple!* and *Emitaï.*[5]

Ousmane Sembène was born on January 8, 1923. As of May 2001, this date was still featured on his identification documents, including the passport that was issued to him in the previous month, in April 2001. But according to Sembène, this is *not* his actual date of birth, as he confided to Djib Diédhiou, an editor at *Le Soleil,* the major local newspaper, in November 1993, on the occasion of the celebration of his 70th birthday.[6] He was allegedly born eight days earlier, at the end of 1922. Now, does this minor, even trifling discrepancy really matter? Not really, on the face of it. But one has to situate these facts within their proper historical context: in 1923 the very existence of a birth record for a native of Ziguinchor, entailing an entry for the exact day, month, and year, was so unusual that it cannot go unremarked. With the exception of the four full-fledged *communes* that were Saint-Louis, Dakar, Rufisque, and Gorée[7]—whose natives were entitled to French citizenship following a bill that was passed in 1916 as a small token of gratitude from France, to thank the natives of Senegal for their war effort—Casamance, like nearly all other parts of French West Africa, was subjected to the regime of *indigénat*,[8] which meant, among other things, that in this colonial context the natives were French subjects who stood on the lowest rung of the social ladder. For these second-class citizens, as in other countries under colonial rule, no record-keeping system was set up to register marriages, births, or deaths. They were only required to have a well-kept and up-to-date income record, the only thing that mattered to the colonial administration.[9] Thus, the very existence of a birth record indicates that Ousmane Sembène was born a French citizen in Ziguinchor, although at the time the area was still a native district. He owes this rather dubious standing to his father, Moussa Sembène, who was born in Dakar.

It seems Moussa Sembène never made much of this "exceptional" status. This Lebu fisherman was quite a character in the native milieu of Ziguinchor in the 1920s. Owing to his bluntness, he was said to be a little "out of his mind." Did he perhaps feel himself, in spite of everything, untouchable on account of his status as a French citizen? Whatever the odds he was facing, he would cross the line. This "rogue," as Sembène one day affectionately called him, never hesitated to speak his mind to the powers that be. Sembène remembers that "one day, the district chief officer came to our neighborhood for a routine health safety control, as was the habit before the start of the rainy season, in anticipation of heavy tropical rains. Upon seeing the shrubs and weeds scattered all over our front yard, he angrily summoned my father and ordered him to pull up these weeds and plant flowers instead. 'But why plant flowers?' asked my father in a sarcastic tone.—'Well, because they're simply more beautiful,' replied the district commander. Then my father retorted: 'I find beauty in my wives, not in flowers.'"[10] A hothead Moussa Sembène certainly was, and a freethinker as well, refractory to any kind of religious orthodoxy or fanaticism. Thus, when he was told that his religious brotherhood, the Layènes,[11] prohibited the use of tobacco, he immediately made allegiance to another sect, less intransigent on this issue. At the time, and given the milieu he was a part of, such types of behavior were inevitably perceived as bizarre and eccentric. But little did Moussa Sembène care whether or not he was up against everybody; he really never made an effort to be accommodating. To this day, longtime Santhiaba residents remember his unflinching attitude during neighborhood meetings. If, at one point in the discussion, someone said to him, "Moussa you're right, but . . . ," he would immediately cut them short: "But me no but, two different opinions can't be equally true. Either I'm right or I'm wrong. It can't be 'Moussa you're right, but . . .'" Sembène puts it all in a nutshell: "My father was definitely crazier than I am." When he talked about his father—something he seldom did—a certain pride and emotion appeared in Sembène's voice, as if he were saying: "See, it's all in the blood, in my case dissent is simply a family affair." Indeed one senses that, in a way, Moussa Sembène made his son in his own image. However, even though Sembène, as we shall later see, was always as wary and headstrong as his father, his artistic temperament was of far greater complexity. He himself conceded as much: "I don't know how to explain this, I just know that in my own special case, I was born free."

In 1923 Ziguinchor, a colonial city enfolded like a pearl within the heart of the Joola country, was already an administrative center. When, in 1645, Portuguese explorers took possession of the area, about 43.5 miles from the mouth of the Atlantic, they encountered the Iziguichos, the local inhabitants, a Baïnouk clan from the Kabos of Jibelor. The Iziguichos are a rebellious community whose history is punctuated by episodes of heroic resistance against foreign invaders.

According to Jacqueline Trincaz, the suffix "or" in the language of these natives means "territory" or "domain," hence the initial name *Ezeguichor*, which eventually evolved into *Sigitior* (under the influence of the Portuguese), before everybody finally settled for the current French spelling, *Ziguinchor*, used here.[12] However, there is another version, according to which Ziguinchor may be a Creole word resulting from the combination of the Mandingo word *sigi* (to sit down) and the Portuguese *tiora* (to cry, to weep). The novelist Boubacar Boris Diop suggests that the name could come from the alteration of *sinta bu tiora*, which eventually gave *Sigitior*. In both cases, *Ziguinchor* would thus mean "sit down and cry." This latter explanation of the origin of the place name, however popular it is, has aroused little academic interest, although it is resonant with the distant and painful echoes of the transatlantic slave trade of the seventeenth century.[13]

Ziguinchor was, according to Jacqueline Trincaz, up to the Portuguese occupation, the hub of "intense trade activities consisting mainly of wax, animal skins, Blacks and ivory that were swapped for iron, cola nuts, fabrics, crystal, amber, brandy, powder and rifles."[14] But whatever the version that will make it into officialdom, there is no getting over this unquestionable fact: the history of Ziguinchor is strongly determined by its geographic location. In colonial days, setting up a trading post in Karabane, at the mouth of the Casamance River, and then penetrating into Joola country by way of the Atlantic, meant for the French that they could get a slice of the Senegambian cake, a region with a substantial touristic and industrial potential.[15] Moreover, Ziguinchor is located on a strategic main road connecting the city to Dakar (280 miles through Gambia) and that also leads to Cap Skirring, 43.5 miles to the west. The city is also close to Tambacounda—243 miles to the east—and to Guinea-Bissau, 108 miles to the south.

Sembène's Casamance was that of the interwar period, the Casamance "that was annexed to Senegal," to quote the historically loaded words of Abbé Diamacoune Senghor, whose Movement of Democratic Forces in Casamance (MFDC) carries on the tradition of rebellious attitude toward any central authority, which is so deeply ingrained in the Joola personality.[16] This spirit of revolt against the prevailing order also lies at the core of Sembène's work and thinking, as evidenced by the very name he gave to his house in Yoff; *Gallè Ceddo*[17] literally means "the house of the rebel" and gives full expression to a desire for freedom that would be key to Sembène's lifetime achievements.

2

At the Crossroads of Cultures

Lower Casamance is blessed with a variety of landscapes and rich, rain-drenched soil. This has attracted, in addition to traders and colonial administrators, natives from other parts of Senegal. In the early 1920s, Ziguinchor was a bubbling hodgepodge of ethnic groups, religions, and languages (Joolas, Mandingos, Serers, French and Portuguese Creoles); yet this was only a rough outline of the shape of things to come: a melting pot of various regional cultures. "I'll always be thankful for the fact that I grew up in such an environment," said Sembène. "It imbued me with an innate sense of respect for difference. These journeys to the interior of my own country were like journeys from one culture to another. I would leave the Wolofs to enter the Joolas' cultural area; from there I would leave for the Mandingos' cultural territory; and when I checked out of the Mandingo area, I was already entering the Fulani region. This sort of culture hopping enabled me to gain firsthand knowledge about local mores, languages, and lores."[1] Around the time the Portuguese were set-tling in the area, the population of Ziguinchor consisted mainly of Ba-ïnouks.[2] Then from 1886 on, with activities related to the peanut trade be-coming more and more labor-intensive, the region started to attract scores of people from all over Lower Casamance, including the Joolas, who would eventually form the dominant ethnic group. Having come to settle in the city with their altars (*U-Kin*) and clanic totems, the Joolas present two distinctive features: first, they have never been under a monarchy; and second, they have never experienced a centralized administration. This community, at heart egalitarian and attached to individual freedom, has always made it a point of stoically bearing the brunt of foreign domination while preserving its intractable identity. The priest, historian, and militant Abbé Diamacoune Senghor argued that the forced introduction of peanut farming under a cash-cropping system, as well as the threefold imposition of a French administration, Christianity, and Islam, were assaults against the value system of the Joola community. Interestingly enough, belief in the free-thinking, autonomous individual and a visceral attachment to tradition are hallmarks of both the Lebus and Joolas of Senegal. Similarly, members of both ethnic groups are reputed to be as stubborn as an over-worked mule!

Ziguinchor has also attracted Balantes, Manjaks, and Mancagnes from neighboring Guinea-Bissau. But the city owes its cultural complexity to the expansionist populations coming from the north and the east, and so it hap-pened that the marabout-conqueror Fodé Kaba imposed Islam and peanut farming in the land of the Joolas, with the tacit agreement of the French. This religious presence has left deep marks in Lower Casamance, which can still be felt today in a variety of cultural areas, including language. Given the importance of these Muslim missionaries, it is hardly surprising to learn that it was a Mandingo who taught Sembène the Koran, despite a situation that must have been far from simple, even for Sembène: "Our marabout didn't speak a word of Wolof." Yet the fact that Sembène had to leave home every day and go to the house of a man who hailed from a different cultural background in order to learn the Koran was a formative experience; it "both enriched and deeply impressed him."[3]

Moussa Sembène, a Lebu from Dakar, epitomizes the Wolof and Muslim migrant who has moved down south to try his luck in the area. The exact arrival date of these "Northerners" is hard to establish; the small amount of information available only allows us to speculate on the time period and the reasons behind the Sembène family's decision to settle in the southern city. According to oral tradition, the Lebus are originally from the former Futa Toro region, in the northern part of Senegal.[4] Successive waves of conquerors kept them under constant threat of foreign domination, and to this stressful situation some simply preferred exile. The initial migratory waves were primarily southbound, and the Lebus first settled in the kingdoms of Jolof and Kayor around the fourteenth century. Strained relations between their community and the Damels, the reigning dynasty in Kayor, forced the Lebus to move further south, where they settled in the Diander. They later moved east where they founded the rural communities of Kounoune, Rufisque, and Bargny on the Atlantic coast. Moving west toward the Cape Verde peninsula, they founded Tyorum, the first Lebu rural community in that area, between Keur Massar and Yeumbeul. There are good reasons to believe it is thence the Lebus reached the westernmost parts of the peninsula (Yoff, Ouakam, Hann, and l'Anse Bernard), the site of Dakar as we know it today. Under the leadership of Dial Diop, the Lebus wrested their freedom from the despotic Damel Amari Ngoné Coumba and proclaimed the independence of the peninsula in 1812.

Saër Sembène, Ousmane's paternal grandfather, was one of the first Lebus to settle in Mboth, known today as Dakar Plateau, the economic hub of the capital. Saër Sembène was a fisherman, like every dyed-in-the-wool Lebu; he also owned cattle and some tracts of land. The latter were located on the current site of the Clarisse hotel, today better known as the Hôtel des députés (Hotel of representatives), at the very heart of the famous Sandaga market. There is a strong suggestion that Moussa Sembène did not settle in Ziguinchor to escape poverty; rather, he came in search of new experiences and in order to fulfill the desire to hold his own. Besides, Sembène's father steadfastly refused to look for any job that his French citizenship entitled him to and that would have eased his way in this prospering harbor city. Moussa Sembène passed down to his son the Lebu's instinctive mistrust toward *buur* (authority). How many times since his return to Senegal, upon the country's independence in 1960, did Ousmane Sembène decline the leading positions he was offered by the Senegalese administration, especially during Senghor's bi-decennial presidency (1960–1980)? There is little doubt that he was then following in his father's footsteps: "My father has always refused to work for anyone; he used to tell me that he'd never be any white man's employee. He just kept on fishing so as to maintain his independence and provide for his family."[5]

In Ziguinchor, Moussa Sembène settled in Santhiaba, on the outskirts of the port area of Boudodi, the residential district where the French and the Lebano-Syrian expatriates lived, which was dubbed *Ebëbë* (White city) by the Africans. The area's setting is gorgeous and readily lends itself to flights of poetic imagination, but Ousmane Sembène was then mainly struck by the gulf between these two worlds, the world of the white settlers and that of the Black natives. The world of rich people could only be seen from a distance, and he would later convey this aloofness through his fictional mouthpiece Oumar Faye, in *O pays, mon beau peuple!*: "The Boudodi residential district could be seen from the distance, its silvery roofs glittering in the twilight of sunset." Facing Boudodi was Santhiaba, the small native town where Sembène was born. Here is Santhiaba, with its adobe huts and squalor, the native area deprived of any water or power supply system, as described by Oumar Faye: "The same paths unfolding before the traveler's eyes like a peacock's tail; the straw huts, always on the verge of collapse; the heaps of refuse: here converged all the loose strands of a teeming social organism."[6] This was the setting where Ousmane Sembène's childhood took place, "where two worlds lived side by side without understanding each other, lived on the same earth, under the same sun, at the rhythm of the same seasons and yet in spite of all this, they didn't share anything together."[7]

Moussa Barro, Sembène's friend and schoolmate at Santhiaba's primary school, remembers Moussa Sembène as a pious man who was held in high regard by the Wolof population. He had built a red-brick, three-room house with a corrugated roof that stood as a powerful symbol of his social success and notoriety. When rare visitors from distant countries come to inquire about Sembène's past, Marie Dia, his elder half-sister, proudly shows them around the property. "This is the three-room house," she will say to you, holding her head erect, "and to this day the building has withstood men and the wear and tear of time. It has remained unscathed." I will never forget her nostalgia-tinged eyes as she showed me one of the rooms, announcing in a high-pitched tone: "*Fii la sama rakk Usmaan juddoo!*" (This is where my brother Ousmane was born!).[8] According to Marie Dia and many inhabitants of Santhiaba, the house does not owe its longevity to the resilience of the building materials alone. Legend has it that Moussa Sembène, on his deathbed, declared that, with the exception of his children, whoever dared make any change to the house would die a sudden and violent death.[9] Souleymane Ndiaye Dimitri, Marie Dia's son, who told us this anecdote, is the current manager of the Aliin Sitooye Jaata stadium in Ziguinchor. This nephew of Sembène's is all the more convinced of the supra-natural power of his grandfather as he has always heard people say his illustrious ancestor was a man feared for his boldness and crude frankness. Surely, he must have benefited from the protection of "superior forces." Whether or not it was due to this curse, the building is still visible on Santhiaba's main road, and it is very nearly the same as what Ousmane Sembène was born in almost a century ago. After Moussa Sembène's death, the house was sold more than once to various buyers. Aliou Sembène, one of the writer's half-brothers, allegedly sold it first to a religious dignitary named Chérif Boubacar, who in turn sold it to one Aziz Haïdara. Youssouf Seydi, former chairman of the Chamber of Commerce, is the person to have purchased it most recently.

This house is primarily the locus of childhood memories, speaking volumes about the man and the artist: it betrays Sembène when he wants to keep, through his stubborn silence, whole episodes of his past under a tight seal, including his relationship with his father. Theirs was a complex relationship, as can be sensed in the stories Sembène confided in 1993 to Djib Dhiédiou during an interview for *Le Soleil*. A complexity that is perceptible in one of the numerous and sometimes conflicting versions of the story of his expulsion from school. The adolescent was reportedly expelled following an altercation with his school superintendent, the Corsican Paul Péraldi, who compelled his native students to sing in . . . Corsican! This was out of the question for Sembène. After the chauvinistic educator slapped him in the face for refusing to oblige, he reportedly struck back with a mighty blow to Péraldi's head. When he learned about the incident, Moussa Sembène, against all Sembène's expectations of getting a severe punishment, simply told his son that he was proud of him. In Moussa Sembène's opinion, one could also get a good education outside the classroom—besides, for him there was no better instructor than life itself. "After my expulsion from school," confides Ousmane Sembène, "my father took me with him on his fishing journeys and, quite naturally, taught me how to fish and smoke a pipe."[10]

Often, the novelist and movie director playfully claims a certain "impurity" of origin, a way of highlighting the diversity of his cultural heritage. This "Joola with Lebu blood"[11] flowing in his veins was breastfed by his Serer mother who was a native of Kahone, a town in central Senegal that is small in size but huge in terms of historical significance.[12] Matar Sène, Sembène's grandfather on his maternal side, was part of the first migratory wave of the nineteenth century, when Serers moved south and eventually reached Casamance, fleeing the Muslim invaders coming from the north. Like every true native of Kahone bearing the patronym Sène and thus belonging to the Serer ethnic group, he was deeply attached to traditional cults, especially to the totemic figures, the *tuur*.[13] The lizard is the totemic animal of Matar Sène's clan. Accordingly, a makeshift altar was set up for the deity in the trunk of a mango tree, which still stands majestically in the middle of the Santhiaba compound. During our conversations, Marie Dia repeatedly pointed out to me that young Ousmane *did* bask in the universe of these ritual practices enacted on behalf of the *tuur* and was even, at the time, assigned the crucial task of cult servant. Every Friday, he was supposed to place at the foot of the altar a calabash filled with curdled milk intended for the ancestral spirits. However, and true to his atavistic irreverence toward the divine, little did the young Sembène care about living up to this lofty liturgical task, and instead of feeding the ancestral deities, he would drink the whole offering and thus leave them empty-bellied. But for all that, the ancestors, no doubt amused by such a piece of mischief, took it easy and never held a grudge against this impertinent worshipper.

Under the protective eye of his *tuur*, Matar Sène gave birth to two sons, Latyr and Ibrahima, and two daughters, Diodio and Fatou. The latter gave birth to Ousmane Sembène's maternal grandmother, another Diodio, who married Alioune Ndiaye, a native of Saint-Louis residing in Marsassoum. Ousmane Sembène is the only child resulting from the short-lived union between their daughter Ramatoulaye Ndiaye and Moussa Sembène. Nevertheless, Sembène has scores of half-brothers and half-sisters on both sides of the parental divide. When his mother left for Dakar, where she married again and founded a new family, Ousmane Sembène was left in the care of his maternal grandmother, who, as is often the case in Africa, did a great deal more toward spoiling her grandson than educating him. It is arguably from this early, surrogate relationship with his grandmother-cum-mother that springs Sembène's great devotion and deep affection for women, as evidenced by his artistic work.

3

Youth and Its Discontents

Since early childhood, Ousmane Sembène has been an incorrigible vagrant. "I needed some space, being always in the same place used to wear me out in the long run. . . . I learned a lot through my childhood experiences. I learned languages and dialects that I would put to good use, four decades later, when I traveled around the continent. I never felt alienated at all. I would stop at any given village and after a couple of hours, I would get me a guide."[1] The novelist, who likes to indulge in long descriptions of Casamance's luxuriant landscapes, entertains abiding and indelible memories of this fascinating scenery: "Palm-trees and coconut-trees, marsh creeks overlaid with water lilies, with the half-bent trunk of a Palmyra palm wood that served as a springboard!"[2] Sembène is always moved by recollections of his bohemian childhood. He is often quoted as saying emphatically, "Yes, I was very happy at the time!"[3]

Is it because he was raised by his maternal grandmother that the young Ousmane was enjoying a freedom of movement that was quite unusual for someone his age? Given the well-known complacency of grandmothers toward their grandchildren, their "little husbands," as they say in Senegal, especially those children who have been separated from their mothers at an early age, there is every reason to believe that this holds true for Sembène. He had the option of staying with any of three families that were respectively in Ziguinchor, Marsassoum, and Dakar, and as he once said to me, he would go from one to the next throughout the whole year.[4]

Lower Casamance, with its rivers and deep forests, gave Sembène, above all, the tremendous opportunity to indulge in his hobbies, that is, hunting and fishing. The writer gives full expression to his love of nature and, more crucially, of his native land, in *O pays, mon beau peuple!,* where at some point the narrator says of Oumar Faye that he "was deeply intoxicated with nature and would never get enough of it. He saw the light of day in this country; he knew, deep down to the marrow of his bones, that he was also made of this his native soil, his skin was imbued with its flavor. . . . Oh yes, he loved the land, this land, *his* land . . . yes, he adored it."[5] But Ousmane Sembène is also a passionate water-lover, which is not at all surprising coming from a Lebu like him. It is a telling fact that in the '60s, when he was identifying a site for his future house, Sembène chose to settle on the edge of the sea. At Gallè Ceddo, the towering waves of the Atlantic crashing down on the rocks are like so many distant echoes of his childhood in the south, in that native Casamance that Oumar Faye likens to a female lover: "The forest was her mysterious fleece, her knees, her strength and weakness and for a voice she had the wind, the thunder or the soft whisper of the night."[6] This is the reason why it could be argued that Sembène's patriotism is less a theoretical construction than a deep-seated attachment to the land, a theme that runs throughout his œuvre, from his first novel, *Black Docker,* to his last movie, *Faat Kiné.*[7] Oumar Faye, doubtless the character who resembles him most, the mouthpiece *par excellence* of the writer-director, says it better than any other character of Sembène's: "A man's dignity doesn't only consist in having children, let alone in wearing beautiful clothes; a man's dignity is also his native land. . . . Now, what about me? Where shall I find my dignity as a man? Where must I conquer it, if not in the country where I was born?"[8] This unconditional love for the fatherland is the prime motive behind Sembène's decision to return to Senegal for good after 1960, and it is all the more significant that from that point on he never tired of urging his countrymen, whom he met during his countless trips around the world, particularly young African students, to go back home and start fighting for change in Africa.[9]

At school, Sembène was what one could call a hellraiser. The boy was certainly a bright and talented student, and always came up first in French composition; but he had the peculiarity of being at the same time taciturn and insubordinate. Actually, this latter feature of his personality, viz. his indiscipline, is what is preeminently remembered by most of his former school buddies.[10] In 1931, Sembène entered the Escale elementary school (today the Malick Fall High School, named after the Senegalese novelist Malick Fall, author of the francophone classic novel *La plaie,* published in 1967). Among his schoolmates, one could cite Moussa Barro and Doudou Diatta (both would eventually become bank employees); Gorgui Diouf (business agent); François Mendy (school inspector); and, most notably, Soundioulou Cissoko, the legendary kora virtuoso. Among his former teachers, one could mention Jules Charles Bernard, who would eventually become mayor of Ziguinchor; Macodou Ndiaye, first questor of the National Assembly after independence and one-time mayor of Saint-Louis; Daniel Corréa and also Jean Kandé, who was his last teacher in the fifth grade, in 1938.

The circumstances surrounding Sembène's "divorce" from the school system are somewhat unclear and controversial. Moussa Barro argues that Sembène wanted to free himself from a suffocating classroom environment and gratify his burning desire to go out in the wild bush swimming and hiking; but this version is at odds with Paulin Soumanou Vieyra's, who claimed that Sembène was simply expelled on the spot by the school authorities.[11] But between Vieyra's and Barro's accounts, there is a third one that seems to reconcile both. It deserves to be taken into consideration, for Sembène himself takes it up again in one of his first novels, *O pays, mon beau peuple!*: "A book was stolen, and no one knew who had done it. An investigation was carried out, which lasted several days, but since it was to no avail, the decision was taken to punish the most troublesome students, in the hope that the culprit would be among them. Since Oumar knew he was innocent, he refused to meet this unjust fate, and that was when the superintendent slapped him in the face. No need to tell you that the latter was beaten senseless by Faye and that as a result he was expelled from school. . . . Despite the mediation of the elders, Faye was adamant that he would not go back to school, saying he was a fisherman, no more no less, like his father."[12]

Whether he was expelled from school while completing his fifth grade or left of his own accord, one thing at least can be stated for certain: the adolescent Sembène, who was always "at home" in wide open spaces, felt like a fish out of water within the narrow confines of a classroom. In fact, the "Péraldi episode" was only the ultimate act of revolt, the one that was too much. Like Holden Caulfield, that archetypal runaway, Sembène was "born to run," as "The Boss" Bruce Springsteen would later sing. He would ditch school and then seek refuge at the house of Moussa Diégane Barro, the father of his buddy Moussa Barro, and he would stay there for days, for fear of being severely punished. At times, he would even totally disappear from the city without letting anyone in the know. This aroused some concern among his folks, who would then scour the native settlements in search of him. Later, he would confide: "I didn't hesitate to set out alone on the journey from Ziguinchor to Dakar, which lasted then four days . . . but I wasn't really alone, for I would get hired as a cook on the ship connecting the two cities."[13]

Many a young girl must have secretly prayed that he never return to the neighborhood. Indeed, as if he were enacting some grim bedtime story, the bad boy from Santhiaba was always on the lookout for any young girl on her way back from the well to give her a hell of a bad time. Marie Dia still remembers those terrible ambushes: "Ousmane was terrorizing us. He would knock down the buckets in which we were carrying water, he would flog us . . . he was such a mean bully."[14] But in spite of this testimony, one must not forget the extraordinary complicity between brother and sister. Marie Dia is the elder sister who has always been dear to Ousmane. In a sense, she was a substitute for the mother whom they seldom saw. This originary lack could explain the prominent place occupied by the mother figure in Sembène's work. Indeed, when he asserts that "God is not a father, God is a mother," one could, in the strict sense, speak of a "deification" of the mother. A case in point: in a room that has been turned into a kind of private museum of African art, the rare visitors who are allowed into Gallè Ceddo can take an admiring look at Sembène's personal poster collection, which includes pictures of Patrice Lumumba, Che Guevara, Amilcar Cabral, Samori Touré; but it is a telling fact that the framed picture of his mother, Ramatoulaye Ndiaye, authoritatively overlooks all these famous figures, however essential they may be to Sembène's personal mythology, as if he were telling these anticolonial heroes: "I love you all guys, I'm sympathetic to all your struggles, but there is no way I'm going to prefer you to this old woman over here. . . ."

If Sembène looked up to these men as role-models, it is mainly due to the fact that, beyond their political decisions, they did not accept the prevailing state of affairs and dearly paid the price for that. The least that can be said about this identification is that Sembène was well prepared to understand their revolutionary stance: he always found himself going against the grain of things. Already in his early age, people thought he was possessed by malevolent spirits (*jin*). His grandmother Diodio Sène was so convinced of this that, according to Marie Dia, she sought the help of reputed *marabouts*[15] in a desperate attempt to exorcise the demons preying on her grandson's mind. What is most interesting in all of this—and made the Sembène problem all the more difficult to solve—was that this little devil of a kid enjoyed the secret and almost knee-jerk admiration of his father! But in a way, Moussa Sembène had struck a bargain with his son and circumscribed the latter's space of autonomy. Sembène sums up this rather unusual situation thus: "My father didn't scold me for my misconducts, but he used to tell me this: 'I can let you do whatever you want, except stealing and lying.'"[16] Rather than send him to the Centre de réhabilitation pour délinquants juvéniles (Rehabilitation Center for Juvenile Delinquents) located on the island of Karabane—and at one point that possibility was seriously considered—Ousmane Sembène was "transferred" to Marsassoum[17] and thus entrusted to his great uncle Abdourahmane Diop. This would be a major turning point in Sembène's life. Abdourahmane Diop, who had settled in Marsassoum in 1922 in order to open the first French language school, was a truly exceptional man, like most French teachers of that period. According to Sembène, "he was an intellectual in the real sense of the word, he wrote in both French and Arabic."[18] Under his tutelage, Sembène would be initiated into the magic world of knowledge. He was already sensing that mental journeys were far more exciting than physical ones, whether in the enclosed world of Casamance or in unknown, distant worlds much further away than the familiar *bolongs*.

Meanwhile, Sembène never managed to withstand the gravitational pull exerted over him by his great uncle. "He had a teaching method all his own," remembers Sembène, "he almost never inflicted punishments but he knew how to bring you to tell the truth. For him, sincerity was the only thing that really mattered."[19] Abdourahmane Diop's religious fervor was so outstanding that the village's mosque was eventually built within his compound. Everyone admired his moral uprightness. At times, he would receive sums higher than his regular monthly salary, and he would immediately return the overage after bringing the Treasury's attention to this little mistake. To what extent did he exert an influence over Sembène on this particular aspect? Things are not so simple as they may seem. Sembène's relationship with money has given rise to wild speculations about his excessive love of it, his thrift and, above all, his intransigence when it came to business matters. But most people forget that nothing came easily to this man, that he always had to work hard to eke out a living or, at times, to earn hardly enough just to get by—as we shall see later when dealing with his Marseilles period. It is quite normal for such a man to be averse to squandering, ostentatious display and the rather snobbish and bourgeois pretense of being above crass materialist concerns. There is no denying that Sembène would go to any length, even fight tooth and nail, to get his due, but this does not only apply to matters where his personal interests were involved, for it is the same principle that governed his relationship with various movie crews. Indeed, those who worked with Sembène on his movies or in other projects readily acknowledge the fact that he always stood by his pledge in financial matters. It is hard to understand Sembène if one does not bear in mind the fact that for all the world fame and acclaim of critics who hail him as one of the finest and most perceptive contemporary African intellectuals, he still stands for the worldly common sense of ordinary people, and this feel for the plain sense of things helped him more than once work his way out of certain contradictions. For instance, in spite of his inflexibility, Sembène often adopted a cynical, quasi jubilatory attitude toward money. Thus, he repeatedly declared, on and off the record, that he was "ready to sell his soul to the devil" in order to find means of making a single movie. One must perhaps draw from this the implication that ethics in the "usual" sense, as Abdourahmane Diop certainly understood it, was for Sembène relevant to and of considerable import in the real world only. Where his dear art was at issue, he was willing to make allowance for any compromise so as not to waste the opportunity of exerting his right of free speech.

It must be added that Abdourahmane Diop was deeply imbued with a strong sense of duty and justice. "When we were kids," said Sembène, "my grandfather never took his meals before the rest of the family. He first saw to it that everybody had their belly full. He explained that for a family head to be entitled to inflict punishments, he must first perform all his duties."[20] Sembène drank deep from the source of inspiration his great uncle represented. He gradually came to the realization that work could be a liberating, self-enhancing factor. When he was only 14, Abdourahmane Diop encouraged Sembène to make himself useful during the busy period of the millet harvest. He also suggested to the children that they sell the grain residue to earn some pocket money. It was his way of bringing home to them the point that dignity only consists in the ability to meet one's own needs. Sembène, who for the first time in his life was thus able to buy his own clothes, never forgot this lesson. Regardless of their expression in the individual or the group, Sembène always held in deep contempt these two phenomena supposedly typical of developing countries: alms-begging and its psychological corollary, the dependency complex. To these issues he devoted a long feature, *Guelwaar,* the story of Barthélémy, now a French citizen, who returns to Senegal to attend the funeral of his father, Pierre Henri Thioune, known as *guelwaar* (an aristocratic title meaning "the noble one"). Based on a true incident, that of a Christian mistakenly buried in a Muslim graveyard, *Guelwaar* subtly dramatizes, without ever lapsing into didacticism or spiteful satire, the divisions, tensions, and suspicions between religious communities in Senegal caught in the psychological maze of neocolonialism and its attendant ills. At some point in the movie the eponymous main protagonist bursts out, in a voice seething with anger: "One pointed finger indicates a direction, but five fingers extended toward a passerby, that's plain alms-begging! If you want to crush a man, give him every day what he needs to survive, for in the end you shall turn him into a slave, not a man. This humiliating attitude of the alms-beggars we are reduced to in this so-called North–South cooperation is slowly killing the little dignity that is left in us."[21]

To counter the commonplace ideas entertained about African solidarity, Sembène repeatedly gives one example in the form of a worst-case scenario elucidating the pitfalls of community solidarity: if the neighbor's house is burning, everybody must lend him a hand to put out the fire and help him, in whatever way, hang on for the first two days or so, but after that everybody must leave the unfortunate neighbor alone; he will have to recover from this disaster all on his own. Coming from a man who claimed to have remained faithful, in spite of everything, to the communist ideology, this line of thinking may sound rather inconsistent to some. One is left to wonder how Sembène could hold together these two divergent threads: an unwavering loyalty to communism, on one hand, and a staunch, rugged individualism, on the other. The latter is pithily expressed in one of his favorite Wolof proverbs: *alalu golo sa lex ba!,* meaning literally "the monkey always has his goods stuck on his cheeks!" In a free translation, this means: "To each his own, what belongs to me is mine and nobody else's, there is no way I'm going to share it with anybody!" Paradoxically enough, Sembène also claimed to have come to writing and, eventually, to filmmaking, out of "love for his neighbor."[22] It would be misguided to cast doubt on his sincerity. Surely, these are disconcerting paradoxes, but they are not half-truths.

In Marsassoum, Ousmane Sembène was assigned the weekly task of fetching water from the well for the purpose of the Muslim believers' ablutions. This entailed countless comings and goings from the well to the mosque's huge earthenware jars. "Since Marsassoum I hate all the Fridays of the good Lord," he sneered.[23] But one suspects that Abdourahmane Diop's piety left deeper marks in Sembène. In fact, it was the Muslim scholar who taught him to revere the written sign. Sembène readily admitted that he valued more his novels than his movies, although the latter brought him world fame: "Personally, I prefer literature. . . . Cinema turns us all into dumb-heads. . . ."[24] Sembène's father also contributed, in his own special way, to this primacy of the written word over the image. Although he could neither read nor write, Moussa Sembène used to bring his son scraps of old newspapers found on the street. According to Paulin Soumanou Vieyra, as soon as he returned to Senegal after independence, Sembène set out to collect and preserve all the manuscripts, both in French and Arabic, left by Abdourahmane Diop. This noble gesture will not come as a surprise to anyone who has heard Sembène talk about his great uncle. More than the army or the world of working-class people, the retired schoolteacher of Marsassoum was Sembène's great mentor and real guide into the larger world. Besides, Fate, through another ironic twist of hers, had it that a similar legend was contrived to account for Abdourahmane Diop's own expulsion from school: he also reportedly gave his school superintendent a sound beating.

Despite his worldwide fame and the respect he has earned from many for a lifetime of struggle, Sembène is also reputed to have been too unaccommodating, even uncouth and stiff-necked. He struck some as being full of conceit and disrespectful toward others. He may have even traumatized his friends and collaborators. For Jacques Perrin, from Galatée Films, who co-produced *Guelwaar* with Sembène in 1992–93, the latter's name certainly brings back very bad memories of their collaboration.[25] The fact that Sembène often made himself insufferable through his behavior should be certainly deplored, but it should be noted that he was conditioned, through his upbringing, to be wary of what he contemptuously called the "Wolof state of mind," which is usually associated with guile and a readiness to strike a compromise on anything or to settle for the easy way. On this score, Sembène was a storehouse of anecdotes that he never tired of telling anyone who bothered to lend him an ear. "One day," he recalled, "a neighbor asked me to run an errand for him, and he promised a reward for it. When I came back, he simply threw a coin at me, for whatever reason I can no longer remember, saying that I didn't deserve it. Well, I gave him his money back, and that's when he followed me on my way back home and complained to my uncle about my alleged misconduct. After listening to both sides of the story, my uncle not only told me I did the right thing, but he also congratulated me."[26] However, one must refrain from believing that Abdourahmane Diop never or seldom meted out punishments. After all, he was a man of his time, firmly convinced that bodily punishment had a virtue of its own. Moreover, Sembène was so obstreperous that sometimes Abdourahmane Diop had no choice but to get rough. Indeed, whenever he deemed it necessary, the old man would get hard on his little devil of a nephew. "One day," remembers Marie Dia, "Ousmane disregarded my grandfather's injunction never to swim in the river; when he came back, Abdourahmane Diop had him tied to a bedpost, and were it not for the intervention of our grandmother, his wife, he would have no doubt spent the whole night in this uneasy position."[27] According to Marie Dia, "as soon as he was untied, Ousmane had nothing else better to do than go back to the river."[28]

In his mature years, Sembène was no less stubborn than he was at that time. This put him sometimes in rather funny situations. For instance, an eyewitness told us a revealing scene that took place in 1998, in the Presidential Palace, where the former president Abdou Diouf was donating computers to all the laureates of the Grand Prix du Président de la République pour les Lettres, Senegal's highest literary prize. In the waiting hall, all the recipients were quietly sitting on their chairs around a table. Now, what was the first thing Ousmane Sembène did as soon as he entered the hall? He simply sat on the said table, which collapsed under the weight of his body. Fellow writers rushed to help him get up but Sembène coarsely pushed them back and made himself stand on his two feet again. No sooner was this done than he sat back on the same table . . .

As already mentioned, the other major influence on Sembène was that of his father, Moussa Sembène. However peculiar was his character, he placed great value on one's word of honor. Sembène remembered seeing him more than once unsettle interlocutors who were keen to reach a compromise by letting out a blunt: "No, there can't be two truths at the same time!"[29] But beyond these two close relatives, Sembène was, in a sense, only the product of a whole generation of men and women who were guided in their actions by strong moral values. Sembène spoke admiringly of them, and went so far as to say, in a grippingly terse formulation: "They didn't want to be mere 'witnesses.'"[30] In other words, they never accepted the cozy blanket of "neutrality" that history kept throwing in their faces and, more importantly, they were not afraid of assuming their responsibilities, even if this meant putting their life on the line.

So it is not inaccurate to claim that Sembène attended the school of hard knocks, and for such a man, who had to learn things the hard way, it is second nature to sense weakness in any emotional outpouring and to be even suspicious of love and friendship. When Sembène claimed that the first thing he would do, upon getting out of bed every morning, was to say the following prayer to God: "Lord, I beseech you to protect me from my friends; as for my foes, I'll take care of them!," one may think he is joking, but he really meant it, to some extent. As we shall see, in his case the loftiest feelings toward the Other were not without a smack of that instinctive fear of being fooled that is the hallmark of those who have been dealt a hard fate.

Léopold Sédar Senghor, who was in a sense the foe Sembène loved to hate and his antithesis, fantasizes about the "Kingdom of Childhood" that he (Senghor) celebrates and idealizes in his poetry. Even though Casamance is no less luxuriant and inspiring than the Serer country, located in what was once the Kingdom of Sine, from where comes Senghor, one would be hard put to find similar lyrical outpourings in Sembène's literary work. Surely, he could have rested content with conjuring up memories and images of a land where everybody is righteous and the landscapes are beautiful. On the contrary, Sembène writes in the same critical vein as the Cameroonian writer and novelist Mongo Beti. Thus wrote the latter in a 1953 review of Camara Laye's novel *Dark Child:*[31]

> As for our dear Camara Laye, he gleefully wallows in the quagmire of banality and exoticism. . . . In spite of appearances, Laye goes out of his way to show us a stereotypical—and thus false—image of Africa and Africans: an idyllic universe, naive optimism, stupidly unending revels. . . . On the other hand, Laye is obstinately blind to facts of far greater import, those that have been always carefully concealed to the French public. This Guinean novelist, my colleague, who was once, if one must take his words for it, a young man brimming with energy and life, can it be that he saw nothing else but a quiet, beautiful and motherly Africa? Can it be that he never once witnessed one, just one of the shameful deeds performed by the colonial administration in the name of civilization?[32]

Most of the time, Ousmane Sembène simply chooses to evoke memories of the native land that has been the setting *par excellence* of colonial injustice and violence. It is this Casamance that makes it possible for the director of *Emitaï* to declare, without batting an eyelid: "I *am* this ambiguous Africa, her past fascinates me and her future exalts me."[33]

4

Colonial Violence

Oumar Faye's return to his native land is one of the key moments in *O pays, mon beau peuple!* On the ship bringing him back home, he is gradually sinking into a nostalgic mood, his heart heavy with longing and his mind all fired up by bitter-sweet memories of the past. He cannot remember the beauty of the landscape without thinking of the violence and injustice that have plagued the city of Ziguinchor, in a context of colonial violence Frantz Fanon describes time and again in the insightful analyses of the chapter "On Violence," in *The Wretched of the Earth*. Like his brothers, Faye is sick of living under the iron rule of a foreign power. This stand against injustice is wholly Sembène's, for it is one of the cardinal values on which his exemplary life and brilliant work are grounded. According to the writer-director, the salvation of African peoples lies *only* in their desire to set themselves free.

Casamance's tradition of dissent, from whose well Sembène drank deep, goes back to the earliest contacts between that region and the West. From 1645, the year the Portuguese administration set up an outpost in Ziguinchor, to the present day, Casamance has experienced three centuries of active resistance (1645–1952) and 49 years of passive resistance (1952–2001). And by a curious coincidence, as if fate were again weaving another thread into the pattern of his life, Sembène was born almost the same year as Aliin Sitooye Jaata, the historical figure who best epitomizes the congenital hatred felt for slavery in that part of Senegal. Aliin Sitooye Jaata was born in 1920, in the colonial district of Oussouye. In the collective psyche of Casamance natives, and of all progressives in Senegal, this young queen, a former *bonne* (housemaid) in Dakar, remains an emblematic figure of colonial resistance during World War II. Many schools and other public institutions throughout the country have been named after her, including the City Stadium of Ziguinchor and the residence hall for women on the University of Dakar campus. According to contemporary accounts, one day in Dakar the young maid had a vision in the Sandaga market: strange voices enjoined her to go back to Casamance and free her humiliated and oppressed people from foreign domination. Once back in Oussouye, she incited the populace to stand up against the colonizer. In 1940 she organized a popular resistance against the excessive taxes levied by the French as "contributions" to the war effort. Jaata eventually became the archenemy of the colonial administration and in 1943 she was sentenced to ten years in prison.

Yet in one respect Jaata was only one in a long line of political martyrs. Decades later, Abbé Diamacoune Senghor started making the headlines as the spearhead of another resistance movement, the MFDC (Movement of Democratic Forces in Casamance). Also born in Oussouye, in 1928, Senghor is regarded by many as the historical leader of this guerrilla organization that has been fighting for the independence of Casamance since the early '80s. To this day, the secessionist claim is a vexed issue for many proponents of the nationalist myth in Senegal, inasmuch as Diamacoune and his followers question the very validity of what they call the forced integration of Casamance into the national territory of Senegal.

In *Emitaï* (1971), Sembène celebrates this forgotten epic of resistance and its unsung heroes, the people of Casamance, thereby making a powerful statement as to the strong hold that the fabled "Queen of Kabrousse"[1] also had on his artistic imagination. Based on a real-life incident, *Emitaï*[2] dramatizes the tension between villagers in Casamance and French soldiers during the early days of World War II. The Vichy government has sent colonial troops to collect taxes and enlist all the able-bodied men in the army. The Joola people will not have it, especially the rice-farming women, who are rounded up to force the village leaders to reveal where they have hidden the rice supplies. This dramatic situation escalates into tragedy, as colonial repression gets out of control. The movie's final image, showing African colonial soldiers shooting at firing range the male leaders of the revolt, was censored in France. Because it also exposed the complicity of Africans in their own oppression, the movie was also banned in Senegal and other parts of Africa.

Moreover, is it not tempting to imagine a chance encounter, during their childhood, between Aliin Sitooye Jaata and the future filmmaker at the corner of a sandy street in Ziguinchor, Bignona, Oussouye or perhaps in the vicinity of some sacred wood? Ousmane Sembène came to the world only three years after the so-called "pacification"—the usual euphemism for violent conquest and subjugation in colonial newspeak. This was doubtless a terrible period. For the colonizer it was simply a matter of subduing for good a population that from 1886, the year Casamance was "integrated" into the French colony of Senegal, to 1917, had been challenging and undermining his authority. The period 1917–1920, corresponding to the so-called "Phase of Implementation of the Brunot Plan," represents a bloody chapter in the history of Casamance, as colonial repression gradually turned into an orgy of atrocities. Richard Brunot, senior colonial administrator, had devised this "Final Solution," down to its last detail, before sailing back to France. Captain Binquet, his successor, took it upon himself to implement this extermination plan putatively meant to "pacify"—one should rather say "lay waste to"—Lower and Higher Casamance, and the Balantacounda as well. In January 1927, Henri Maubert, the infamous colonial administrator, had some natives shot dead in Ziguinchor, on a spot where today the memorial to the heroes of resistance in Casamance is located. According to the official version, the executed natives were guilty of cannibalism—prohibited in AOF[3] and AEF[4] after a decree was issued in April 1923. In actual fact, the motto by which these insurgents lived was: "We'd rather die free than live like slaves."[5]

Nowadays, when Casamance's resistance against the French occupation is evoked, most people tend to remember the refusal of Joola farmers in 1942 to pay taxes, in the form of rice and canon fodder, levied by the colonial administration. What is less known, and this is something that Abbé Diamacoune Senghor often pointed out during our conversations, is the fact that in Lower Casamance "everything was different from what you had in other areas. Here farmers were beaten and humiliated and they were made to pay more taxes than others."[6] According to the militant priest, Casamance was subjected to six forms of tax collection: in addition to cash and soldiers, the region also provided rubber, cattle, rice to feed soldiers on the front, and even honey, since there was a shortage of sugar in France.

It was not the first time Casamance natives were refusing to be involved in a so-called world conflict that did not concern them at all. They had expressed the same sentiment during World War I, leading to the famous visit that Blaise Diagne, who was then Senegal's representative in the French Parliament, made to Ziguinchor on March 6–8, 1918. In 1917, France was in dire need of "fresh troops" to strengthen its ailing regiments on the northern front. To this end, and in order to prevent any popular uprising as in previous enrollment campaigns in Africa, Blaise Diagne, freshly appointed "General Commissioner of African Troops," came to encourage the natives to enlist in the army. He was copiously insulted and even slapped in the face by a young Joola girl—who was eventually sent into exile. History textbooks, including those written in Senegal after independence, seem bent on overlooking this resistance or of denying it its due historical significance.

Peanut growing was another major point of contention. The forced introduction of an export-oriented farm product could only exacerbate the tension between natives and the colonial administration. For the Joolas this implied, above all, the destruction of the forest, which is doubly sacred in their culture insofar as it provides the means to their livelihood and is a source of spiritual nourishment. However, there is a third reason accounting for this strong dislike that is seldom pointed out: during the Middle Passage slaves were fed with peanuts. Thus, for such a freedom-loving community the peanut is the very symbol of a wretched condition, that is, slavery.

In Lower Casamance, Ousmane Sembène experienced firsthand this colonial violence. He also attended Blaise Diagne's political meetings in Ziguinchor. His father, Moussa Sembène, was a highly respected dignitary in the city, and the meetings took place at his house. Says Sembène, looking back on those times: "I was already bearing witness, unawares, to major events."[7] In 1938, Baye Wélé Sembène, Moussa's junior brother and a construction worker in Dakar, came to take the young Ousmane to

Dakar. Was this second "transfer" caused by Abdourahmane Diop's death one year earlier? A cloud of mystery still hangs over this question. In any case, for Sembène this marks the end of a period and the beginning of a series of new and formative lifetime experiences in the Lebu milieu of the "Big City."

PART TWO

DAKAR: THE TURBULENT YEARS

Overleaf: Ousmane Sembène during a stay in the
United States, 1989. *Photo courtesy of Thomas Jacob.*

5

The Lebu Ghettos of Dakar Plateau

Ousmane Sembène did not leave Ziguinchor with a light heart. Even though he had developed an intense passion for adventure, such a journey to the unknown, at only 15, was bound to raise some apprehensions in the young man. His uncle Baye Wélé Sembène felt that his nephew was indeed a bit hesitant, and that was the reason why he came in person to make the trip to the capital with him. When Sembène arrived in Dakar in 1938, the outbreak of the Second World War was only months away. He took up residency in Thiédem, one of the city's oldest neighborhoods, at 45 Rue de Thiong. His elder sister Faat Sembène also lived in the same house, which was that of their aunt Rokhaya Guèye. Sembène's extended family members are mainly fishermen and landowners; it is a wealthy Lebu family, not in terms of possessing material goods, but in the sense that its name and line of descent confer upon its members a certain prestige. Recall that when he was 8 and later on, Sembène regularly "ran away" to Dakar whenever he felt in a wandering mood.

At the time, Rokhaya Guèye was still living on Rue Paul Holle. But Sembène saw how colonial authorities gradually confiscated all the lands belonging to the Lebus before handing them over to the trading companies from Bordeaux, Marseilles, and other major French port cities. The increasing need to protect all these interests gave rise to a tentacular administration that took up a great deal of space for its offices and the accommodation of civil servants. Under these circumstances, the land issue soon became a top priority on everyone's political agenda. The French did anticipate the risk factor that mass displacement entailed, and thus they proceeded according to a well-wrought plan. Some lands were confiscated but sometimes compensations, often ludicrous, were granted. When Sembène eventually left for Europe in 1946, he would by then have come to the bitter realization that the Lebu community of Dakar Plateau was coming apart at the seams, that it was driven out of the city center and into the outskirts, causing its members to be scattered all over the peripheral native districts of Dakar. In 1938, Rokhaya Guèye's house on Rue Paul Holle was leased to Scarpita, a French company, and the same fate would later befall the house of Saër Sembène, his paternal grandfather. According to a typical pattern, Sembène and his relatives were thus forced to leave the Plateau and settle in the Medina. The wretched shack in which he lived with his sister Faat Sembène was pulled off the earth and transplanted in "Native Medina," the Tanga-Sud of all colonial cities in Africa.[1] It would be quite a bit of a stretch to evoke the Native Americans in connection with the mass displacement of these populations; however, one could speak of "Lebu reservations" in Mboth and Thiédem, in Dakar Plateau.[2]

This situation also gave young Sembène the opportunity to go through new experiences. From 1938 to 1944, his life in these two neighborhoods was punctuated by *kasag*[3] under the supervision of the *selbé*,[4] *ndawrábbin*[5] parties and spiritual songs with his religious brotherhood, the Layènes. He also enjoyed once again the sea and discovered comics and cinema.

Although he was an only son, Sembène had scores of half-brothers and half-sisters on both his paternal and maternal side. In Dakar he found this extended family and rediscovered his own father's childhood. Maurice Ousseynou Fall, one of Sembène's lifelong friends, said he often met him on Rue Paul Holle during summer break.[6] Maurice and Ousmane played together in these old "native"[7] neighborhoods, and the young Sembène made then quite a few other friends: Baye Ali Paye, Alhadji Touré, Doudou Guèye and his older brother Abdoulaye Guèye, Mokhtar Ndiaye, Gorgui Thiaw, Doudou Ndir—who became a boxer before sailing for Marseilles where he would stay until his death—Moustapha Diouf, older brother of the great journalist Bara Diouf and the late Ibrahima Sow. It is perhaps worthwhile to dwell a bit on one oft-overlooked aspect of Sembène's formative years. Counter to a belief propagated by Sembène critics, especially Paulin Soumanou Vieyra and Françoise Pfaff,[8] Sembène *did* have a second chance after his expulsion from school in Ziguinchor. Upon his arrival in the capital in 1938, he was enlisted in the fifth grade at the *Ecole de la Rue de Thiong*. Maurice Fall, one year his junior, was among his fellows. Sembène hated school, all the more since the sandy beaches of Gorée were just a stone's throw away from where he lived . . . There was so much more to learn on the streets of Dakar, symbol of colonial power and where France had established the headquarters of AOF in 1902. Why put up now with a colonial educational system he had already fully rejected when he was in Ziguinchor? At the end of that school year in 1938, Sembène did not even bother to take the graduation exam marking the completion of his elementary studies with a CEPE (elementary school degree).

But Sembène felt drawn to the ocean for another reason: he could dive into the sea to retrieve from its depths the coins tourists would throw overboard to watch with amusement the swimming feats of young city boys. At the time, Dakar was a major harbor, and this prominence was compounded by the fact that all the trips between Europe and Africa had to be undertaken by boat. The port was astir with commercial activities. Assane Samb, son of Rokhaya Guèye, who lived in the same house as Sembène, on Rue Paul Holle, was then the "big shot" of Môle II (Jetty Section II). This stalwart Lebu was Sembène's senior and had a tremendous influence on him. Fearless and physically impressive, Assane Samb was the type of person to whom authority came naturally. With him Sembène could earn some money doing odd-jobs of a more or less legal kind. This also enabled him to indulge in his two great nocturnal hobbies: reading comics and going to the movies.

However, Maurice Fall claims that Sembène dropped out of school a long time before the examination period for the CEPE. In any event, one fact remains indisputable: Thiong, where he left his mark as an irregular and troublesome student, was the last stage in Sembène's incomplete elementary education. Even though his new comrades admired this unruly boy, his command of the French language being far above average, it was a helpless issue: money, not the degrees earned after years spent droning the lessons one toiled to learn, was what fascinated Sembène. In Ziguinchor he came to realize that money was empowering, and at this moment in his life Assane Samb, also known as "the rugged man," became Sembène's model—Maxim Gorky would have to wait for a while. Years later, Sembène would explore this theme of the power of money in the feature film *Mandabi*, released in 1968 and adapted from his novella *The Money Order*.

This landmark movie, the first ever made in an African language, tells a simple story: a man receives a money order from his nephew in Paris and attempts to cash it. But at the Post Office it all starts taking on Kafkaesque proportions, as our hero, Ibrahima Dieng, realizes that first he has to go through a lot of red tape, courtesy of the former colonial administration. The order, it turns out, has thrown his life out of order, and Sembène brilliantly exploits this situation to sketch a satirical portrait of the corrupt, money-crazed *petite bourgeoisie* emerging in the wake of Senegal's independence. In a famous scene, Ibrahim Dieng's second wife, Aram, improvises a paean to money that perfectly conveys this *zeitgeist: Ku ne xaalis neexul da nga koo amul; xaalis amul reen wànte ci xol lay sax* (Only the penniless deny the pleasure gained from money; money has no roots but it grows in our hearts).[9]

However, this obsession with money was already spreading like a disease in the '30s, and in such an environment Sembène, ever the independent-minded, plotted an escape. Like a caged bird, he sought ways to spread his wings and follow the "call of the wild." "It was in 1938," remembers Maurice Fall, "Ousmane Sembène and I had just made it to the school's entrance; it must have been the end of the school year, for all the students were feverishly preparing for the CEPE exams. But on that morning, Ousmane Sembène was entertaining other projects. I saw him turn back and head for the harbor. When I later asked him about this strange behavior, he simply whispered into my ears: '*Médie II.*' *Médie II* was the name of the French commercial ship that was regularly operating between Dakar and France. Every time he was told about the ship's arrival, Sembène would ditch school."[10]

If the harbor in Dakar was a source of income for Ousmane Sembène, the sea—water in general—was a real passion for the clique of "troublesome and idle"[11] young Lebus he was hanging out with. These adolescents were sea people, and they would while away their time playing games and wandering around Teeru Baay Sóogi, the famous beach located on the Corniche Est (eastside cornice), behind the Presidential Palace; they would take a plunge at *grass bu ndaw* (smaller beach), near the Marine (French Navy base) and at *grass bu mag* (greater beach), near the pier of the Dakar-Gorée launch. Ousmane Sembène and water, it is an old love story. During the numerous trips we made together over the years, I often heard him complain about the lack of a bathtub in his hotel room. "I like to splash about in the water," he confided to me. His Lebu atavism, no doubt . . . According to Vieyra, Sembène was prone to seasickness, a claim that the latter has always denied. In addition to his wanderings on the edge of the sea, Sembène's Dakar years were also marked by *kasag* sessions held at the house of Doudou Cissé, who was their *selbé*. These *kasag* sessions, consisting of riddles, songs, dances, and other recreational activities, were a genuine alternative school, not unlike Sembène's celebrated definition of his cinema as an *école du soir* (night school). Beyond the ritual practices related to circumcision per se, the *kasag* sessions were meant to "mold" the mind and body of the young initiates so as to better prepare them for the difficulties of adult life. They were also a means of integrating the individual into greater society, as is shown in Camara Laye's *Dark Child*.[12] Surely Sembène, who was a sensitive young man, did not leave the Sanctuary of Man, that retreat where the circumcised are trained for adult life, the same person. Some traits of his personality were reinforced and, so to speak, brought out in the full light of day through these group interactions sustained over a long period. Would he have become what he is today if it were not for the resulting strength of will needed to overcome obstacles? Sembène may have also, as suggested by the writer and journalist Boubacar Boris Diop, learned to master the art of storytelling during that initiation period. According to Diop, "Sembène has a *selbé*'s state of mind, which means primarily that he is an extremely gifted storyteller; moreover, like the *selbé* he only respects those who have been through hardships, for he himself had to toil for a living, he had to contend with adverse existential circumstances to achieve great things."[13]

According to Maurice Fall, one of the persons Ousmane Sembène admired the most was a wrestler named Soulèye Ndoye, who lived on Rue Raffenel, a couple of blocks away from Rokhaya Guèye's house. Every night Sembène would stand for hours in front of his idol's house in the faint hope of catching a glimpse of him. Soulèye Ndoye was, like most wrestling champions of that time, a consummate artist, that is, he was both a great dancer and a talented *bàkk*[14] singer. Music, gestural poetry, and the cult of bodily strength: all these aspects of wrestling culture explain why for Sembène the "call of the arena"[15] was as irresistible as the mermaids' song.

According to one of his friends, Sembène himself was reputed for his dancing skills. Doudou Guèye points out, with a cunning smile, that he was particularly fond of the *yaay a ma yónni* (meaning literally "it is my mother who sent me"), a furious music that the coolest among the youth of the '30s were rocking their bodies to. Rokhaya Guèye herself had gained some notoriety in the neighborhood as a great dancer, and some even say that she had no match when it came to the *arwatam xaañ ma ci,* a dance in which great emphasis was placed on eroticism.

Wrestling, music, and dancing . . . Ousmane Sembène basked in the same cultural environment in the youth organization L'étoile du destin (The star of destiny), created and so named by Mokhtar Diop, an operator, mechanic, and metalworker. There was at the time a host of youth organizations consisting of men and women of the same age group. At the head of each organization were a male head and a "mother," that is, a godmother or a female patron. In the case of L'étoile du destin, they were respectively Niakhane Paye and Sophie Thiam. The house of the latter served as a kind of "headquarters" where the young men and women would congregate after school or work. In that house were held rehearsals for cultural events such as the *fanals.*[16] Here is what Doudou Guèye remembers from these meetings at "Mother Sophie's": "In those social groups, every girl had a lover, but it was all about platonic love, itself subjected to a strict code of conduct. Thus, for instance, the selection of lovers took place in public. Every boy would throw his hat or beret on a pile and the girls, who knew to whom each one of these headgears belonged, would take their pick."[17] With such a prudishly symbolic language, the privacy of everybody was preserved. The next day, the girl would start knitting a pocket handkerchief bearing the initials of her "Charming Prince." Thus was officially sealed the love relationship, and Doudou Guèye is keen to stress another point: "It was all innocuous, very pure. The girls' virginity was sacred, and at dusk they would all go back to their houses."[18] The old man does not say it openly, but he clearly seems to be thinking, with a pang of regret, that times have changed. They have, indeed!

It was during those years that Ousmane Sembène fell in love with poetry. He confided that he continued to write poems to any woman he happened to be enamored with. This wooing technique, which is rather unusual for the cold Sembène most people know, lends itself perfectly to a man who, surprisingly enough, always acted shy in the presence of women. Mokhtar Diop's observation confirms this feature of Sembène's personality: "When we're among us, Sembène was hilarious; he kept the conversation going and was cracking jokes all the time. But as soon as there was among us a single girl he wasn't well acquainted with, he started paying attention to what he was saying, became more reserved and showed much respect and care for the girl. In fact, Ousmane was no longer himself during those moments."[19] As far as feelings are concerned, Sembène was never able to entertain a long-term relationship. After two divorces, he "settled for" loneliness. The only permanent female figure at Gàlle Ceddo was Nafi, the devoted housemaid who had been working for him for more than 20 years. Withdrawn into himself, the novelist became enclosed in a private world inhabited by women who were the figments of his imagination, who were created according to his own ideal of femininity, who could not interfere with his work because they were precisely part of it. "My work is absolutely incompatible with the presence of a woman," he said, "sometimes I may wake up more than once during the night because an idea came to my mind and I must commit it to paper to make sure I'll later find the same words describing the same idea. Also, when I come across some interesting stuff during the day, I park my car and watch the scene. No, my work is too consuming to leave room for any kind of interference."[20]

In fact, Sembène's inclination for loneliness goes back to his childhood in Casamance; in Dakar it only became more pronounced. While leading a normal life in the capital, Sembène never missed an opportunity to enjoy the simple pleasure of reading. Not surprisingly, the future writer-director could not do without either comics or movies. He would emerge enraptured from these activities, for they carried his imagination to distant worlds. According to the testimonies of his friends during that period, Sembène would then become an altogether different person, especially when he was reading. They all describe a quieter, more relaxed Sembène, literally transfigured by the adventures of *Cassidy, Zembla,* or *Captain Miki.* Unfortunately for Sembène, the stories were often published in serial form and thus he was always dying to know what happened next but could not afford to buy the following issues. He would then be seen prowling around the Plateau looking for the young Lebano-Syrians who were bound to have the needed issue. Sembène was fully aware that he owed a huge debt to these youth readings: he firmly believed in their educational value and saw to it that his youngest son, Moussa, never lacked them.

Yet in spite of this marked preference for the medium of writing, Ousmane Sembène remains, in the eyes of critics and the public, the "Father of

African cinema." Likewise, this second passion did not come out of the blue; it too goes a long way back to his childhood in Casamance. In Ziguinchor, his father would often give him money so that he could go to the movies. This may sound trivial nowadays, but at the time movie theaters were regarded as temples of vice. Hence this curious "Senegalism" that speaks for itself: *bandit-cinéma* (movie-thug). Was Moussa Sembène a "visionary" or was he merely following his anti-conformist bent? In any case, he did not feel that by encouraging Sembène to go to the movies he was exposing his son's "innocent" soul to some satanic influence. In the late '30s and early '40s, the Dakar metropolis gave Sembène the opportunity to observe almost every day his movie-going ritual. The movies he saw had such a strong hold on Sembène's imagination that he soon named all his friends after movie people and characters. Gorgui Thiaw was dubbed "Eric" after the famous Austrian actor and director Eric von Stroheim—and the moniker has stuck with him. Sembène called Ibrahima Sow "El Kébir," his nephew Chérif Dia "Django," the archetypal cowboy who enjoyed a great popularity among Senegalese movie buffs between 1960–1970. But beyond these anecdotes, it must be noted that, by a strange coincidence, Sembène discovered cinema in 1938, that is, at the very time that it was becoming an integral part of the urban culture of colonial cities in Africa. The "seventh art" was introduced in Senegal in 1900 with a screening of *L'arroseur arrosé* by the Brothers Lumières—of course, it was exclusively intended for Europeans. Then movie theaters were built for those labeled "natives." After the transition from silent to talking movies, cinema gained in popularity and became increasingly profitable for movie companies—all French, of course—such as the Société d'Exploitation Cinématographique Africaine (SECMA) and the Compagnie Africaine Cinématographique Industrielle et Commerciale (COMACICO). But for colonial authorities, cinema was above all a tremendous propaganda medium. There were many movie theaters in Dakar before World War II, including the Rex, on Avenue Faidherbe and the Rialto, an outdoor movie theater on the current site of the West African Central Bank headquarters, owned by Maurice Jacquin.[21] Today all these movie theaters have been replaced by commercial centers, which are mushrooming all over the huge bazaar that the Senegalese capital has become over the past years. To have lived during that period enabled Ousmane Sembène to see how far behind African cinema is lagging today, a delay he attributed to the lack of any real cultural politics, whether in any individual country or on the continental level.

Although the colonial administration was successful in promoting a movie industry, one must not forget that it always brought its exclusionary mechanisms to bear on its policies. The Palace, a movie theater that was owned by one Maurice Archambault, located on the former Rue Béranger Féraud, was strictly reserved for whites, who were mainly working for trading companies such as Chavanel, Peyrissac, or Maurel et Prom. Another movie theater, the Plazza, was likewise for whites only. Racial segregation, which was commonplace in all the colonies, was also exacerbated, in the specific case of cinema, by pricing policies. But Sembène was too young to take offense at this stupid arrogance of white colonials; he was entirely consumed by his newfound passion. Outside the normal screening hours, Sembène could be seen standing in front of the billboards, lost in his reveries and oblivious to the rebukes of the old women selling peanuts at the entrance, who became increasingly concerned about his future and his moral integrity. In those days, the El Malick offered two daily screenings, priced at 50 cents per screening for westerns. Sembène remembered viewing in that movie theater *Bouboule, 1ᵉʳ roi nègre,* directed by George Milton, shot in Dakar and featuring Pape Demba Dia, the pioneering Senegalese actor, in the title role.

One day, Sembène was nearly "killed" at the Rialto. "Coin-fishing" at *Môle II* was a risky and ungainly affair; it was always a miracle if one could fish out the coins tourists would toss into the sea when the ship was nearing the bay. Thus the kids were sometimes compelled to gatecrash in order to enter the movie theater. Maurice Jacquin, the owner, would punish those he caught red-handed by holding their heads under water in a huge barrel. This disciplinary measure had a strong deterring effect on the more timorous ones, but Sembène was not the kind to be easily cowed by these scare tactics. The day he had the terrible misfortune of being caught, Sembène's punishment was all the more severe since he was rumored to be the leader of a gang of young thugs purposefully creating a chaotic situation at the entrance the better to help gatecrashers sneak in and attend evening screenings. In a way, these kids, out of frustration with the tediousness of their daily lives, were somehow playing in their own "movie." Their rambunctiousness was only the inarticulate expression of their desire for another world, another life, and the westerns they saw on the screen summed it all up, in their typically simplistic way: "A lonesome cowboy, gunshots and a hero always narrowly escaping from perilous situations. Handsome and strong, our hero always ends up defeating the outlaws and earning the passionate love of a maddening babe that is sealed in the apotheosis of the final kiss. So intoxicating is the eternal seduction of westerns. . . ."[22]

Nineteen thirty-eight was also the year of Sembène's first momentous movie experience: *Olympia,* by German filmmaker Leni Riefenstahl. In this film documenting the 1936 Berlin Olympics, Hitler is shown leaving the stadium to avoid having to shake hands with Jesse Owens, who had won four gold medals in a single day (for the 100 m, 200 m, long jump, and 4×100 m relay). The main purpose behind the screening of the documentary in Dakar was to turn public opinion against Nazi Germany. According to Paulin Soumanou Vieyra, with *Olympia,* Sembène started to gain awareness of race as a concept and of racism as a social phenomenon. What seems beyond doubt, however, is that Leni Riefenstahl gave him a sense of the expressive power vested in the image.

But his uncle Baye Wélé had not brought this young man all the way from Ziguinchor to Dakar to escort him through the utopian worlds of Gorée and the American far west. Baye Wélé was a construction worker and Ousmane Sembène was supposed to be his helper. Sembène was soon to face the harsh realities of a worker's life, thus beginning a new episode in his personal story.

6

The World of Labor

In Ziguinchor, Moussa Sembène had already introduced his son Ousmane to the world of labor. "At night we used to go carp fishing. It was cast-net fishing, and the dugout had to glide slowly on the water. We had to row without making the slightest noise. Sometimes I would fall asleep, on and off, then my father would throw fish bait in my face and stuff me a pipe to fight off this drowsiness."[1] *O pays, mon beau peuple!* is resonant with echoes of these evenings on the river: "The dugout was moving westward, under the melancholy glow of lonely stars. The paddles stroke the water at a rhythmic pace. Along the shore mangroves were eerily silhouetted against the melancholy twilight of the nascent evening. . . . Their eardrums were abuzz with the surrounding silence. . . . Carps, mullets and other fishes were strewn all over the rear end of the dugout. The moon rising above the landscape spread its opalescent sheet over the riverbed."[2]

In Dakar, however, there was neither Casamance River nor gorgeous landscapes for the construction helper. Ousmane Sembène was then only 15, and most of his comrades had a far better start in life than him. Some of them entered the Pinet Laprade Vocational School, others were hired in the colonial administration. Among his friends, only Niakhar Paye, who lived on Rue Valmy, maintained contact through the years. As a worker in the '40s, Ousmane Sembène took part in the construction of numerous public buildings that are the pride and glory of present-day Dakar. In 1941, he was part of the team commissioned to build the Van Vollenhoven High School—today the Lamine Guèye High School—under the leadership of Boubacar Diouf "Rafet,"[3] a construction foreman and head of the Masonry Department at the Pinet Laprade Vocational School. During the same period, Ousmane Sembène took part in the building of the Bloc des Fonctionnaires (Lodgings for Civil Servants). Located near the building of the Centre des cheques postaux, the Bloc was used to accommodate overseas civil servants, doctors and teachers who were assigned to the civil service. Today the complex, which in recent years has come to be better known as the Bloc des Madeleines, serves an altogether different purpose: it hosts the District Court and the Division des Investigations Criminelles (Bureau of Criminal Investigation), the infamous DIC that Abdoulaye Wade's political adversaries consider to be an all-powerful secret police deploying its far-reaching tentacles to keep them in line.[4] Even though the DIC is no KGB, the former Bloc is no Holiday Inn, and those who are interrogated inside its premises know that all too well. This location, where indignant democrats in Senegal regularly converge to vent their anger at the State, is, ironically enough, also the "work" of a certain Ousmane Sembène!

The next five years spent as a construction helper under Baye Wélé Sembène's supervision were exhausting. During this period, Ousmane Sembène experienced both the limits of his own self and the lot of "the wretched of the earth": physical overwork and injustice. The feeling of being unfairly exploited is reflected, in Sembène's case, in the estrangement from a number of his relatives on the paternal side. In the house of his boss Baye Wélé, he felt like *the* undesired one. Everybody in the house regarded him as a good for nothing and an unnecessary additional burden on the household's limited food resources. A hopeless case indeed, this son of Moussa Sembène's: too dumb to become a civil servant and too full of himself to turn into a submissive worker to be used and abused at one's will. Sembène was the only member of his work team who did not receive his salary every other week.

Baye Wélé kept the money under the pretext that he provided free room and board for the young man. In order to raise enough money to at least cover his movie tickets, Sembène had to fall back on expedients. He had to sell empty cement sacks to peanut street vendors and did not think twice about doing part-time work as a *baay jagal*.[5] This term could be rendered as odd-jobs man, but in Sembène's case it was mainly about collecting scrap iron or any other used object from houses in his neighborhood and selling them in various junkshops. Sembène's knack for recycling goes back to these hard times when he was ready to do anything to make ends meet. At the headquarters of Filmii Doomireew, his production company, costumes and other antiquated accessories were stored in a junkyard, waiting to be "recycled" for future movies. Nothing was to be discarded. One day, as he was talking about the state of African cinema, Ousmane Sembène drew on the collecting/recycling metaphor, explaining that "to make a movie in Africa is like collecting cigarette butts to roll a full one." *Borom Saret* (The horsecart driver) is a good example of this creative process. This short feature, which marked Sembène's entry into the movie world, was made with an old Russian camera and scraps of film gathered here and there.

In addition to his activities as construction helper and handyman, Sembène also did a short stint as a mechanic at Hunebelle before being drafted during World War II. Hunebelle was located at the intersection of Rue Sandiniéry and Rue Blanchot. The automobile was gradually becoming a part of the Dakar urban landscape and the mechanic Hunebelle, father of the world-famous actor James Hunebelle, was something of a celebrity in the capital. Thanks to this initiation into mechanics, Sembène would eventually be assigned to the transportation corps of the 6ème Régiment d'Artillerie Coloniale (Sixth colonial infantry regiment) in Niamey, Niger. Although all these formative experiences took their toll on him, they also helped him better understand the noble values inherent in work, of which he says in *O pays, mon beau peuple!* that it is the contribution each of us brings toward the well-being of all. Speaking of his experience as a construction helper, Sembène readily waxes nostalgic: "Yes, I have been a construction helper in this city, and to this day when I pass by one of the houses I helped build I sometimes wonder if the people who live in them are happy. . . ."[6] For Sembène, there is nothing nobler than a willingness to make oneself useful to the community. But when some individuals want to exploit this community work for their own gains, one must always take a principled stand against that. In Sembène's personal case, one must take note of the crucial fact that the exploitation of his labor power first took on the human form of one of his close relatives, i.e., his uncle Baye Wélé. Thus, Sembène's fight against injustice would always be associated in his mind with an oppressive African family structure, the abuses of birthright and, in a larger historical context, a certain feudal mentality. Later on, he would readjust his rebellious gaze and trade the axe of this sweeping rejection for the double-edged sword of a revolt against, on one hand, a political system controlled and corrupted by foreigners and, on the other, the overwhelming pressures and demands of African society.

However, no account of Ousmane Sembène's youth could be comprehensive without giving due weight to the colonial context, which was deeply marked by a policy of racial segregation and in which were embedded the precarious lives of the inhabitants of Mboth and Thiédem during and after World War II.

7

The Experience of Racism

Spatial organization has always been the most telltale feature of colonial racism. But if Santhiaba, the "native" district in Ziguinchor, was something like an outgrowth, a collateral effect of the European settlement, things were altogether different in the Plateau of Dakar. It is perhaps worthwhile to say a few words about the history of the current Senegalese capital, to put things in perspective. The debate on the etymology of Dakar is still raging. The autochthons still call it *ndakaaru*. Historian Assane Sylla, drawing on the findings of linguists specializing in Dravidian languages, argues that the word derives from the Tamil *nakarou*, meaning "town" or "city."[1] The Bengali origin of the family name *Mbengue*, a typical Lebu patronym, is often brought up in support of this argument. Others claim that *ndakaaru* may have originated from a nasalized pronunciation of *dëkk raw* (house of peace, safe haven). It is also worth noting that according to various scholars, including Cheikh Anta Diop, the Lebus are said to be the descendants of a Nile Valley ethnic group that ancient Egyptians called "The Peoples of the Sea." After crossing the Senegal river in the course of successive migratory waves, they stayed for a while in Walo and Djolof,[2] before settling for good on the Cape Verde peninsula around the middle of the sixteenth century. A Moor scribe named the place Dar-el-Salem (House of peace), which the Lebus translated as *dëkk raw,* and which would eventually evolve into Ndakaaru and Dakar. However, according to Boubacar Boris Diop, there are two other versions. The first is that Dakar comes from *dax-aar* (tamarind tree), owing to a legendary confusion: a European asked the inhabitants about the city's name and the latter replied by telling him the name of the tree they were sitting under. This is why, argues Diop, in Cheikh Hamidou Kane's *Les gardiens du temple,* Dakar was fictionalized as *Tamarine.*[3] According to proponents of the second version, one Daccar, a French military officer, gave the city his name. Each of these different accounts has its supporters, but they all corroborate the fact that the Lebu settlements of Mboth and Thiédem predate the arrival of Europeans in the Cape Verde region. True, the latter already knew their way around the coasts, with Gorée as a landmark. The Dutch transformed the island's Lebu name, Béer, into Goode Rade (Good harbor), which eventually gave Gorée.

Gorée was a hotly contested strategic site coveted by all the European colonial powers, on account of its location two miles off the mainland. After successively falling into the hands of the Dutch, the English, and the French, the island was "definitively" recognized as a French possession through a treaty signed on May 30, 1814, in Paris. From now on, the Lebus would feel a new threat hanging over their frail Republic, founded in 1790 after centuries of struggle against Kayor. The Lebu community was born out of a relentless quest for freedom, as is shown in Abdoulaye Sadji's small collection of sea stories and legends, *Tounka;*[4] and as the prospect of another foreign domination was looming large on the horizon, they prepared to face these new invaders—come from afar this time.[5] As for the French, they were emboldened by their total control of Gorée and Saint-Louis and felt that the time was ripe to take over the Cape Verde peninsula, an area far larger than Gorée, and use it as their entry point into the interior. For the Lebus this was the beginning of the end, an "ominous dawn" that Cheikh Hamidou Kane vividly captured in *L'aventure ambiguë.* However, the complete annexation of Dakar and the ensuing loss of the Republic's independence on May 25, 1857, did not involve any "blood and tears" tragedy. Negotiations were held that led to the signing of treaties, but that did not make any difference, as

Kane put it in his novel: "The result was everywhere the same: those who fought and those who surrendered, those who compromised and those who doggedly stood their ground, they all found themselves, at the end of the day, numbered, scattered, classified, labeled, drafted, administered."[6]

After the 1857 treaty, it was only a matter of time before the Lebus would be gradually and irreversibly deprived of their whole heritage. There ensued, according to historian Assane Sylla, "a gradual acquisition of lands by the French military, the civilians and the Gorée traders, either by purchasing them or through a lease contract, and sometimes through land seizures, with the usual provision of compensation for losses."[7] The more Dakar was being urbanized, the more the old Lebu settlements lost sizeable portions of land—and to such an extent that they were reduced to a tiny enclave set right in the middle of the white city. Of course, the cohabitation with Lebanese expatriates, French civil servants, and sailors from all over the world was anything but easy. According to Bara Diouf, "this native neighborhood was situated in the heart of posh-looking, 'whites only' and urbanized Plateau: more than an eyesore, it was an anachronism. This Negro village, in whose narrow confines Ousmane Sembène and all the young Lebus of his generation had to live, had sharply delineated borders in a perimeter formed by Rue Raffenel, Rue de Thiong, Rue Paul Holle, Rue Sandiniéry and the William Ponty, Gambetta, Faidherbe and Pinet-Laprade avenues."[8] Hence the development, at lightning speed, of the Medina, as a sort of demographic dumping area located on the outskirts of the Plateau and intended for Lebu families like Sembène's, migrants from the interior, and thousands of farmers fleeing the rampant poverty now plaguing the countryside.

Whites-only brothels on Rue Raffenel were also part of the Plateau's urban landscape during the '40s. *Cocottes* (prostitutes) brought from France were supposed to give some "moral" uplift to their "blood" brothers (French, English, and American). Further, owing to the presence of thousands of soldiers, Dakar was to become a stronghold of the Vichy regime. But for Sembène, the real issue was segregation against the Negroes, at the very moment when the latter were shedding their blood to defend the "fatherland." This was racism in its most primitive and irrational form, and it would leave deep scars and painful bruises in the minds of a whole generation. The journalist Bara Diouf speaks eloquently of this situation: "This was Dakar under the Vichy regime in the 40's: a beleaguered city bearing the brunt of inflation, shortages and, above all, the nearly hysterical racism of a large community of French expatriates held hostage in Senegal. It was during this period that for the first time I heard someone call me 'nigger' and 'darky,' the period when I awakened to the bitter-sweet feeling of Otherness. I must add that this feeling was shared by most young people in the Plateau."[9] There is a sequence in *Camp de Thiaroye* where this state of mind is vividly captured, and Sembène will often return to this scandalous situation, deliberately occupying the vantage point of the eyewitness. Firmly convinced that "colonialism always kills twice," Sembène considered the rehabilitation of its victims to be of paramount importance. Alluding to the countless massacres perpetrated in the name of colonialism that current revisionists either try to conceal, downplay, or explain away, he further clarified his thinking: "We can forgive, but we must not forget. We have a duty of memory to fulfill, we must recall these facts that colonial historians have always attempted to sweep under the rug."[10] However, it was only later in his life that Sembène would gain a keener awareness of the colonial situation. During World War II, he was simply not well equipped to resist, let alone challenge, the Juggernaut of official propaganda. For a reason that its inhabitants themselves could not grasp, Dakar had become a high-stakes area in the fight between the Axis (Germany, Italy, and Japan) and the Allied Forces. Appeals to patriotic feelings were thus particularly insistent. On October 15, 1939, the Senegalese representative Galandou Diouf published in the newspaper *Paris-Dakar* a fiery open letter to Black fighters and the population of French West Africa (AOF): "You're fighting," he told them, "not for the sake of Poland, but for the civil rights that were dearly paid for and are now threatened. . . . If we incur the misfortune of losing this war, it is not Paris that Germany will lay claim to, it will be the colonies, it will be *us*. This is why we must fight this war."[11] The point was simply, as can be seen here, to demonize Germany. Religious leaders also played their part by praising France's "moral" qualities. Prayers were held in the mosques and on January 18, 1940, Abibou Sy, son of El Hadji Malick Sy, said to members of the Tijaan[12] religious brotherhood: "I hope that the civilized nations striving for a world of peace will side with France and its allies to wipe this abominable people of Germany off the face of the earth."[13] One can easily guess what school textbooks looked like, as they were also pressed into the service of propaganda.

Cut off from the metropole, whose resources were now exclusively destined for the front, Dakar was soon faced with serious economic hardships. The draconian distribution of rice, meat, sugar, and fuel led to an inflationary situation, with prices soaring high and a thriving black market. Africans were the most affected by the crisis.[14] The dockers in the harbor, the street vendors of Sandaga and Kermel, and numerous industrial workers went on strike. The colonial authority responded with seizures, lay-offs, and dismissals.[15] But there was a far more serious concern for the colonizer: the Black soldiers, exasperated by the racism prevailing in the army, insisted on being housed, fed, and clothed in the same way as their white comrades. The case took on critical proportions, and upon the request of General Garrau, Commander in Chief of the French West African troops, the community spiritual leader Seydou Nourou Tall went to Ouakam, Thiaroye, Bargny, Rufisque, and Saint-Louis to "placate the spirits of the soldiers."[16] The 1940 debacle of the French army and de Gaulle's subsequent call to resistance from London occurred in this context of widespread frustration. Pétain's government, headquartered in Vichy since July 2, 1940, had put for safety in Dakar the finest ships of the French navy, including the Troisième Flotte (Third fleet). Among the battleships anchored in the Dakar harbor, there were prestigious ones such as *Le Richelieu, Le Montcalm, Le Georges Leygues, Le Terrible,* and *La Gloire.* Triumphant Germany was turned overnight from being the demon of apocalypse into the angel of resurrection. Now the devil was cast in the shape of General de Gaulle. Ousmane Sembène was only 17 and it was hard for him to understand what was going on. This is why in *Emitaï* a perplexed colonial infantryman—tellingly enough, the role was played by Sembène—asks his superior, after intently gazing at de Gaulle's picture freshly posted on the wall, how a three-star general can replace a seven-star marshal.

In the fall of 1940, on September 23, Allied planes bombed the city of Dakar. It all started on Monday morning, at 9:00, when tracts inciting the population to overthrow Pierre Boisson, the governor representing the Vichy regime since July 13, 1940, were hurled pell-mell into the quiet Dakar cityscape. Boisson was given four hours to surrender, if he did not want the city to be completely destroyed. While the ultimatum was still running, all the Europeans and the Lebano-Syrians were evacuated to safe areas, but the Africans, citizens or not, were abandoned to their fate. At 1:00 PM the air squadron, consisting of RAF officers and French forces still loyal to de Gaulle, carried out their threat by raining down shells on Dakar. Then all hell broke loose: during the following three days, thousands of native residents in the Plateau flocked to Sangalkam, Rufisque, Diourbel, and as far as Kaolack, some 140 miles from Dakar, to seek refuge in the interior. Sembène and his buddies, still in their teens, had little idea what was really at stake, and all they saw in the general panic was a tremendous opportunity to get free food: "We went from house to house," he confides, his eyes beaming with mischief, "and took advantage of the owners' absence to eat our fill!"[17] The Allied Forces—five battalions of the Royal Marines under the command of Admiral Cunningham—attacked the city with only two fighter planes, but Dakar was defended by no less than four regiments of colonial soldiers and one infantry regiment, as well as by the artillery on the seafront. The English, who allegedly came through Môle I (Jetty Section I), were chiefly interested in taking Gorée Island, no doubt to destroy the *Richelieu*, the French flotilla's finest and most important ship. But confronted with the overwhelming superiority of the opposition, Churchill had no choice but to issue an order on September 25, telling his struggling troops to withdraw. There were 175 dead and 350 injured, almost all Blacks.

The air raid on Dakar left deep scars in Sembène, whose neighborhood was a prime target. For all intents and purposes, this war was making huge demands on him, and for years he would not be able to muster any genuine response to its entailed challenges. It is perhaps for this reason that the theme of World War II would be broached only later in his career, with *Emitaï* in 1971 and *Camp de Thiaroye* in 1988. The latter long feature brought back painful memories, which were forcefully conveyed by the speech that chief-sergeant Diatta made in the Coq Hardi, the cafeteria-cum-bordello that in the movie also serves as a meeting place for war veterans. Thus, even Black fighters could be victims of racial discrimination.[18] As one can easily surmise, Sembène's disarray was that of a whole generation, as Bara Diouf reminds us: "In this new postwar Dakar, the return to the colonial *status quo ante* came as a shock, particularly for young people in the Plateau, living in a state of expectation, as if they were waiting for an explanation; but they also knew that the ineluctable moment of confrontation was drawing nigh. One can really say that at the time a revolt was brewing, and we felt like embers under ashes." With his usual dead-pan humor, Diouf goes on to speculate about what it all may have meant for his generation: "Maybe we, Black people, felt that things had gone too far and, for once, we couldn't have it anymore?"[19] Maurice Fall is not of the same persuasion. According to him, there was not the slightest hint that the youth was becoming more aware of its responsibilities, let alone gaining a budding political consciousness. If it came to pass that Sembène attended meetings of the French chapter of the International Labor Association (SFIO), whose representative in Senegal was Lamine Guèye,[20] then it was more to revel in the atmosphere of hooting, cheering crowds and to hear the drumbeats, than to listen to boring speeches. In fact, Sembène never took politicians seriously, casting them in all his movies as overzealous collaborators of the colonial administration; and there are good reasons to believe that his tendency to side with the troublemakers at those meetings was an early expression of his contempt for slick-talking orators. However, one must not extrapolate: it may well be that Sembène's cynicism already implied an unconscious rejection of politics, but this picture is at odds with the postwar Pan-African militant using his pen and camera as weapons of stinging political critique.

Meanwhile, he found solace in religion and became a devout member of the Layène brotherhood, regularly attending the sessions of religious singing held at the intersection between Rue Tolbiac and Rue Galandou Diouf.[21] Since his childhood years in Casamance, Ousmane Sembène basked in a deeply religious environment. With his maternal grandmother in Ziguinchor, he had lived in the pagan world of the *tuur,* those totemic ancestors he used to cheat of their gifts for his own enjoyment. The childhood years in Casamance were also marked by the Koranic school at the house of a Mandingo marabout; further, at Marsassoum the village mosque was built inside the compound of his grandfather Abdourahmane Diop. But it will not have escaped notice that by that time, he had come to hate all the holy Fridays in the world, as they were associated with the drudgery of fetching water from a distant well. In Dakar, as a member of the Layène brotherhood,[22] he had his hair shaved clean and sang every night, at the top of his lungs, verses from the Koran.

According to historical accounts, it was on May 24, 1884, that in the small Lebu village of Yoff was first heard the "Call of Limamou Laye Thiaw," a native Lebu from Yoff who claimed to be the Mahdi, a divine messenger whose coming was allegedly predicted by the prophet Mahomet.[23] Limamou Laye Thiaw advocated a return to Islamic orthodoxy, faith in the oneness of God and a strict compliance with the teachings of the prophet, including a painstaking and dedicated enactment of the Islamic rites (ablutions, daily prayers, alms-giving, social justice, and the steady invocation of Allah and prayers for Mahomet). Limamou Laye's message was issued in a context where the French had gained total control of the economic resources of Senegal,[24] and the Lebu Republic had lost much of its hard-earned autonomy. The Cape Verde peninsula was also much coveted by the French who had settled on Gorée Island. On October 10, 1826, and April 22, 1830, the Lebu authorities had signed with the French agreements stipulating that the latter were to pay fees for every ship docking in the Dakar harbor. Thus, until 1857, the

Lebu Republic and the French entertained relations as two sovereign states. Then Protet, a French navy officer, took control of the Cape Verde peninsula with a handful of sailors aboard the *Jeanne d'Arc*. One can therefore easily understand why the French felt threatened by Limamou Laye's rallying cry in 1884. It was the same religious movement, come with a vengeance after the air raid in September 1940, that aroused in Sembène spiritual feelings lying dormant in the deeper recesses of his mind.

Until February 1944, Ousmane Sembène played an active role in the brotherhood. He organized nightly religious sessions in the Rebeuss neighborhood, right next to the eponymous correctional facility,[25] at Alassane Djigo's house, a well-known athlete of the time—today the Pikine stadium, in the outskirts of Dakar, bears his name. According to his cousin and friend Doudou Guèye, from 1940 to 1944 Ousmane, "who had shaved his hair, sang at the top of his lungs until the break of dawn during the Layène's religious nights."[26] But this love affair with spirituality quickly turned sour. What really happened in Sembène's mind during those four years? One must refrain from giving a one-sided answer to this question. Maybe his mystical crisis sprang from a trivial act of social bonding: the spiritual leader of the Lebu community, the Seriñ Ndakarou, is also invested with tremendous temporal powers. Moreover, as he was raised by the pious Abdourahmane Diop, Sembène was well prepared to embrace this religious message. However, one cannot rule out the possibility that he found in religion, as later in cinema, a means of escaping the tediousness of daily life. All of this must have carried weight while he was making up his mind, but everything indicates that it was a personal crisis. Beset by contradictory ideas and feelings, Sembène was in search of a middle ground and in the process of constructing his own identity. There was no way he could have remained apathetic to Layène messianism: the coming of the Mahdi had everything in it to fire up his imagination; it was the sign that Islam, born in Arabia, was being appropriated by his own community.

In this respect, the only movie in which Sembène tackles head-on the highly sensitive issue of religion is *Ceddo*, released in 1976. *Ceddo* tells the tale of a pagan king, Demba War, who converts to Islam and allows a Muslim teacher, the Imam, into his circle of advisers. But up to then this royal council consisted exclusively of *ceddos*, a caste of warriors who recognizes the king's sovereign powers *only* in times of war. They resent the king's unilateral decision and openly challenge his authority and the proselytizing enterprises of the Muslim cleric. In the ensuing power struggle, the *ceddos* abduct the king's daughter, Princess Dior Yacine, to compel him to meet their demands. Then the upstart imam, who has been all the while pulling the strings, steps into this political power game and, through deceit and murder, ultimately prevails over the *ceddos,* introducing slavery and racial stigmatization in the community. In this cinematic work, Sembène took the bold step of casting both Islam and Christianity as utterly foreign civilizations that had, for this very reason, similarly nefarious effects on the native culture.

The Layènes, by putting Negro culture at the heart of a religion brought by foreigners, could only elicit an enthusiastic response from him, although at the time he could not articulate an explanation for the magnetic pull African spirituality exerted over him. When on February 1, 1944, Ousmane Sembène was drafted to defend the French Republic, he did not waver for a moment; he was even looking forward to fighting it out with those "abominable" Germans who had dared to despoil his "fatherland." Official propaganda indeed had a far deeper impact on him that he was wont to admit.

8

"Here We Come, Marshal!"

When Pétain, premier of Vichy France, announced the Armistice on June 16, 1940, the colonies received this news as a big letdown, especially in Senegal, the most French of all. People had mixed feelings about this turn of events, and there was a great deal of incredulity, and even shame, involved. France, "Mother of the Arts, Arms and the Law"[1] was now under the yoke of Nazi Germany, that "embodiment of absolute Evil." The rhetoric of imperialist conservatism had hit its mark. Ousmane Sembène, who refused to chant the "Marseillaise," was not the type to be easily deluded into believing that his ancestors had blue eyes. But as Maurice Fall rightly pointed out to me, "every young man was proud to be a French citizen and was lost in admiration of France." After the defeat of the French troops, Dakar sank deep into grief. Prayers were again held in mosques and here is what was written by Mamadou Moustapha Mbacké, a marabout in Touba, the homebase of the Murid brotherhood, to the AOF General Governor: "At a time when our motherland [*sic!*] is going through such a tragic period, I want to reaffirm, on behalf of the whole *Murid* community, my undivided loyalty.... We are ready to make every material or moral sacrifice to save France."[2] Then many young men started to volunteer. According to historian Cheikh Faty Faye, by the end of January 1941, the entire district of Dakar had already given more than 3,170,055 francs to the Secours National (National Relief). The case of a schoolteacher from Rufisque is quite typical of the overly jingoistic mood prevailing at the time. He was an *évolué,* an assimilated, and he felt, like Sembène, that he owed France something in return for having brought stability and "jolted us out of our lethargy." After he was declared unfit to practice the art of war, the schoolteacher asked the Public Treasury to withdraw from his monthly salary 100 francs, a sum representing his personal contribution to the war effort—and this, he insisted, until the final victory against Germany. According to Doudou Guèye, such an extraordinary fascination was quite usual among the so-called *évolués:* "At school, in all our songs, we celebrated the glory of France, her strength and her beauty; they also told us that we were all, whites and Blacks, her children."[3] However, one must always point out that in spite of this ideological drill, France laid claim to her colonial possessions by the sheer force of weapons. But as Cheikh Hamidou Kane reminds us, "when the arm is weak, the mind is at great risk."[4]

So intense was Sembène's love for France that 50 years later it was still remembered by his friends. Maurice Fall told me one anecdote that gives a good idea of Sembène's eagerness to be drafted into the army: "It was one Thursday afternoon, in 1943. We were, as usual, hanging around the *Rex* movie theater, on the Avenue Faidherbe, waiting for an opportunity to see the afternoon movie matinee. There was a vacant lot a couple of blocks away, which kids from a nearby school had turned into a recreational battlefield. That day, Gorgui Thiaw (Eric) was playing with a sling, using pips from a jujube tree as projectiles. One of the sling shots inadvertently hit Sembène in the eye, and as he was writhing in terrible pain, he started to yell out: 'Oh man, my eye is screwed up! Look, he screwed up my eye! Now I can no longer enroll in the army, they won't take you if you're one-eyed!'"[5]

However, this bellicose zeal should not always be ascribed to the patriotism of the concerned. According to Issa Sembène, a native of Rufisque and a former colonial soldier (class of 1940), at the time few young people were aware of their status as French citizens. The war mainly represented for them a tremendous opportunity to achieve their dream of going abroad.

There was of course a great deal of machismo involved, as nobody wanted to pass for a coward: "We were proud," says Issa Sembène, "to be declared fit because those who weren't felt emasculated, and we called them 'sissies.' We all wanted to go to the front to prove our manhood."[6] Those who knew Sembène very well will readily acknowledge that this must have played a decisive role in his case.

The exact date of Sembène's enlistment remains something of a mystery. The required age to perform military service was 20, and accordingly Sembène must be of the class of 1943, not 1942, as Vieyra suggested. It is more plausible that he actually registered on February 1, 1944, the same day as his friend Djibril Mbengue. Why wait one year after the regular date of his draft? The question still hangs in the air, but whatever the reason, a new chapter opened in Sembène's life, and this war experience would radically transform his worldview. "School didn't teach me anything," he would say four decades later, "I owe everything to the war."[7] So on February 1, 1944, Ousmane Sembène, Djibril Mbengue from Rufisque, and Omar Samb from Colobane went to the training camp of the Sixth Colonial Infantry Regiment (RAC) located on the current site of the Camp Dial Diop (military base and army headquarters in Dakar). He became Private Second Class Ousmane Sembène, identification number 689,[8] and stayed until April. The training was intensive, and Maurice Fall could sense that it was taking its toll on his friend whenever he came to visit. Sembène was indeed a little disillusioned when he confided to Maurice Fall: "*mbër fii kekk la, nen du fi bonde!*" (literally: "Dude, this is hard ground, no egg will rebound on it!"). This was Sembène's way of conveying, through this popular Wolof expression, the toughness of life in the army. Recruits were often put in jail any time they missed a day of training. In addition to this tight discipline, which could in no way agree with his rebellious temperament, Ousmane Sembène experienced racial discrimination, like all Black soldiers. He took to watching the twin hills of the *Mamelles* (The breasts) during his spare time, storing images that he would later capture again with his pen, as in the famous opening lines of *Black Docker*:

> *Her face was wet with tears as she gazed after the ship which had just rounded the Almadies—"The Breasts," Senegal's only mountain peaks. Mossy in some places, bare in others, their barrenness made them ridiculous. The savanna was broken up by knobbly, parasitic cacti. The baobabs looked neglected, like twigs shed from a broom. Nature had not gone out of her way to embellish this part of Africa.*[9]

After the training phase, the Sixth Colonial Infantry Regiment was scattered all over the colonies, its members sent to wherever the French flag was still flying. Ousmane Sembène was assigned to the Artillery Annex in Niamey. As a driver-mechanic, he found himself in the same barrack as Djibril Mbengue. Sembène's company had to move whenever a transportation of troops was needed, notably in Morocco—by way of Algeria. During those 18 strenuous months in desert areas, the most difficult times for Sembène, who liked to live near the water, were precisely the lack of drinking water and the constant thirst. Scantily dressed, the soldiers had to reckon with the scorching sand on their bodies and had only canvases to protect themselves from sandstorms. Sembène the driver had to grope his way along without any map, and the colonial soldiers who lost themselves during extended breaks were abandoned to their fate. Issa Sembène and Djibril Mbengue remember this last part, their shaky voices betraying a deep emotion: "When our comrades lost their way in the desert, we didn't bother to look for them, on the contrary we stuck around for three or four days, our eyes fixed on the sky, for only the vultures could tell us how to locate, at the very least, what was left of them."[10]

Unlike most of his comrades, Ousmane Sembène did not enlist again after the mandatory 18 months. But however short-lived it may have been, this experience had such an impact on him that he would later draw on it to flesh out the life story of Oumar Faye, the main protagonist of *O pays, mon beau peuple!* and also, as previously noted, his fictional alter ego. As Faye put it: "Before the war I didn't know a thing, I lived from day to day, my projects vanished with every setting sun. Then I was drafted and came to have putative enemies: the Germans. I was taught to hate and fight against them; I was taught to hold out physical pain; whether it was snowing, hot or cold, one had to fight. I lived side by side with every man from every nation, and we shared the same meals, dodged the same bullets. . . ."[11] His experiences as a soldier are visible throughout Sembène's œuvre, not only in this second novel, *O pays, mon beau peuple!,* but also in movies like *Emitaï* and *Camp de Thiaroye*—not to mention his frequent allusions to war in other works. It is far from a stretch to claim that in the Niger desert, Sembène came to terms both with the meaning of existence and the higher value of man. By living with death or its imminence on a daily basis, he came to realize the futility of some social partitions. The desert, a mineralized, impassively hostile universe, revealed to him the frailty of human nature. In this elemental world, as Antoine de Saint-Exupéry wrote, "a pilot's business is with the wind, with the stars, with the night, with sand, with the sea. He strives to outwit the forces of nature. He stares in expectancy for the coming of dawn the way a gardener awaits the coming of spring."[12]

For Sembène, however, the real break occurred after 1945, during a post-war period that was humiliating beyond anything he could have imagined. "Once the war was over," narrates Oumar Faye, "we wildly celebrated a victory achieved at such great cost. We had just regained that universal freedom meant for all. One day, it was a year after that victory, a man with whom I fought told me: 'Without us what would have become of you, what would have become of the colonies?' That sentence, uttered on the first Day of Liberation, came as a total shock to me. Then everything became clear to me at once: I understood that we had no fatherland, that we were the pariahs of this world. When the others said 'our colonies,' what could we have said, we Africans? The dignity of a man . . . it is also his country."[13]

In 1946, returned without any injury from the war, the colonial soldier Ousmane Sembène was the only one of his class *not* to receive an honorable discharge. In a Dakar astir with great social movements, Sembène eventually broke with the Layènes. At 23, he had only one thing in his mind now: leave Senegal . . . take flight.

PART THREE

DAKAR IN THE POSTWAR PERIOD

Ousmane Sembène during a stay in the United States, 1989.
Photo courtesy of Thomas Jacob.

Tell me why, innocent child,
Why you want to leave our beloved land
For these overcrowded cities
Where you will harvest pain and misery?
Tell me why you want to bid farewell
With pomp and style
To our dear majestic Baobabs?
Over there,
Trembling in the snow,
How you will miss our toms-toms!
And with dreamy eyes you will stalk,
In the foul weather of gray December,
The overshadowing ghosts of trees
Ethereal.

—Ousmane Sembène,
O pays, mon beau peuple!

9

The Winds of Change

Her face was wet with tears as she gazed after the ship which
had just rounded the Almadies—"The Breasts," Senegal's only
mountain peaks. . . . The liner cleaved through the waves. . . .
A large cloud engulfed the setting sun, filtering the reddish
rays, tingeing the sky a deep rust. . . . Far off in the distance,
the trail of smoke imperceptibly vanished into the air.
The floating mass continued lazily on its way until it was
nothing but a black dot.

As one can easily guess, in the above cited opening lines of
Black Docker, Sembène is vicariously on his way to France through the sad
musings of Diaw Falla's mother. In spite of the disappointments and misgivings about France in the aftermath of the war, he was unwavering in his faith
that there, at least, opportunities he was denied in Senegal would be up for
grabs. At only 23, Sembène was already experiencing the hardships of life in
exile, which always implies a double absence: of the native land and of one's
own self. Surprisingly enough, Sembène was going to a country for which

he had started to harbor a deep-seated hatred. Two years before, he thought he was fighting for universal freedom, while in actual fact he was merely strengthening the chains of his own bondage by getting himself involved in the liberation of France. After the return back home, he reminisced about the "long walks in the desert, a knapsack on your back, and during those treks you would accumulate a lot of resentment as you walked on." Maurice Fall confirmed to me this new state of mind: "I don't know what happened during the war, but this wasn't the Ousmane I knew, he had nothing in common with the childhood friend who went to perform his military duty. There was such an anticolonial rage in him!"[1]

The massacre of colonial soldiers in Thiaroye on December 1, 1944, was the event that was most symbolic, in a very tragic way, of the "colonial misunderstanding," as Cameroonian film director Jean Marie Teno calls it. After addressing the issue in *Camp de Thiaroye*, Sembène clarified again his standpoint: "If I keep talking about Thiaroye, it's nonetheless in a very dispassionate way; I'm not harboring hard feelings against anybody or any nation. However, I've to make sure people know my history right . . . these soldiers returned from the war . . . they shed their blood for France and the French didn't hesitate to kill them!"[2] France's attitude was so shocking that even Léopold Sédar Senghor, usually so complacent toward France, could not come up with any excuse for it. Incredulity, disappointment, and anger coalesce in his poetic interrogations:

> *Black prisoners, I should say French prisoners, is it true*
> *that France is no longer France?*
> *Is it true that the enemy has stolen her face?*
> *Is it true that bankers' hate has bought her arms of steel?*
> *Wasn't it your blood that cleansed the nation*
> *Now forgetting its former mission?*[3]

Now, it must be pointed out that once elected president of Senegal, Senghor would never again bemoan the tragic fate of Thiaroye's martyrs. For Sembène the dates are telling enough: while French soldiers were shooting his Black comrades, he was putting his life on the line every day in the Niger desert—and this for that same murderous France!

As a very sensitive and introverted person, Sembène has likewise reflected on countless other events of political import. On August 25, 1944, only seven months after his enlistment in the army, Paris was liberated by the Allied Forces of General Dwight Eisenhower. What role did the colonial troops play in this liberation? The question was posed to Sembène when he came to Rice University, in Houston. Here is what he replied: "When Americans talk about this war [World War II], they only show American soldiers, and it is true that the latter's involvement was decisive. The Europeans also see everything from their own perspective. As for Africans, they have participated in all the wars of this century, but only for the liberation of other nations; it is up to us, Africans, to see to it that the rest of the world knows we have been major players in that great historic event, even though today Europe would prefer to forget this crucial fact."[4] But there was something more scandalous than this deliberate forgetfulness: at the time of the fall and *reconquista* of German-occupied Paris, General Philippe de Hauteclocque Leclerc, once at the gates of the cities, asked Eisenhower to let his Deuxième Division Blindée (Second Armored Division) enter first so that white soldiers could go down in history as the liberators of Paris. Black fighters, hidden away in Fontainebleau, were eventually denied the honor to parade on the Champs Elysées. This was something Sembène deeply resented, and he has always made it a point to set the historical record straight by saying crudely: "*We* liberated Paris." Even though he was not directly concerned by the episode, Sembène uses the word "we," which carries a heavy emotional weight, to refer to all the colonial soldiers from Africa.

What was most revolting for Sembène was doubtless the fact that Africans have never been in a position to say that they were betrayed, as France made it clear very early on that it would not loosen its tight clutch on the colonies. The Brazzaville Conference held from January 30 to February 8, 1944, left no doubt as to France's willingness to reinforce, by any means necessary, its colonial empire. Under the aegis of General de Gaulle, the conference was held in a patronizing spirit strongly reminiscent of the 1885 Berlin Conference, when the fate of Africa was sealed between colonial powers, without Africans having any say about it. The only participants at the Brazzaville Conference were hand-picked senior officials from the French colonial system: twenty-one colonial governors, nine members of the Advisory Assembly, and six monitors sent by the General Administration in Algeria and the General Residencies in Tunisia and Morocco. As Xavier Yacono aptly puts it, "no native from Africa took part in it and only a handful of 'assimilated' sent reports (six actually) that would be read during a session devoted to the issue of family and social customs."[5] The "assimilated" whom Yacono is speaking of were those natives who had reached a certain educational level. Often well integrated into the administrative and economic apparatus, they could not imagine a life outside the orb of colonialism—accordingly, they were its most zealous servants. Their major "political" demand was to be assimilated while being allowed to preserve their native customs. It is perhaps worthwhile, at this point, to dwell at length upon the Brazzaville Conference, for as we shall see, the economic, social, and political paths of development mapped out for Africa were to have a deep impact on the social context prevailing in Dakar, when Ousmane Sembène returned from the war in 1946. It is even very likely that it played a crucial role in his decision to leave for France.

To his enormous credit, General de Gaulle did not mince his words at the opening session. Laying down the "ground rules" of the conference, he said unequivocally to his African audience: "In accordance with the higher ends of the civilizing mission undertaken by France in the colonies, we rule out any possibility of development outside the French imperial bloc; the likelihood of forming *self-governments* in the colonies, even in the distant future, is to be left completely out of the equation."[6] What de Gaulle called "a certain idea of France" simply excluded any emancipatory project for the colonized. They were just granted a token representation in the metropole, in the French National Assembly, but the main point was to lean on the colonial possessions to get France back on its "imperial" feet. To this end, a "production plan" was designed, which advocated a cautious industrialization, through incremental stages, in the colonial territories, with bolder steps to be taken in the sectors of agriculture and education. The plan also recommended an increase in employment opportunities for the colonized and the suppression of the *indigénat* system. The necessity of recognizing occupational groups was also conceded. The term "trade union" was thus eschewed but everybody had it on their minds.

Now, what were the consequences, on the ground, of the Brazzaville Conference? Senegalese historian Mbaye Guèye has shown that the Thiaroye massacre was not an isolated and irrational act, but rather the first outcome of a historical process set in motion in Brazzaville. He went so far as to see in that bloody repression an act of political cleansing.[7] The December 1944 rebellion came as a confirmation that now things would be totally different in the French empire: the postwar period was bound to be rife with revolts. The French state, ruined by the war and humiliated by Germany, could not afford to lend a receptive ear to claims coming from the colonies. The rest is well known: 45,000 people killed in Sétif, Algeria; 100,000 dead in Madagascar; the Algerian war of liberation from 1954 to 1962; and the Dien Bien Phu debacle.

In postwar Dakar, Ousmane Sembène found himself in a completely new political and social setting. But before talking about the social atmosphere as such, it must be pointed out that on a personal level, this "homecoming" was marked by a deep disappointment he was never to forget. Until his departure for the military training camp in 1944, Sembène had lived, as we have seen, on what had been until then the property of his grandfather Saër Sembène, in the native settlement of Thiédem. But Thiédem, upon his return, was like a lingering relic from a dead past, as its tiny social world had completely fallen apart. Under pressure from the colonial administration, the Lebus of the Cape Verde peninsula, including those of Dakar, were steadily losing their lands. But up to then, and in spite of the contingencies of a hard life, Ousmane Sembène had never left the land of his ancestors. Likewise, the arson attacks deliberately perpetrated by the colonial administration in Mboth and Thiédem did not *unsettle* him at all. In 1914, Blaise Diagne, the freshly elected representative of Senegal at the French Parliament, personally intervened and induced Governor William Ponty into officially declaring that "Lebus who were landowners in Dakar and whose huts [*sic*] had been destroyed [by arson] would keep their lands in the city."[8] During his 18-month absence, the house of his youthful years, at the corner of Rue Gambetta and Rue Paul Holle, had been leased to Lebanese expatriates—however affected by the hardships of war economy, Sembène's family on the paternal side was notoriously greedy. It was thus for him a new estrangement, this time from the universe he had grown up in as a kid, away from the places that had shaped his character and imbued him with a sense of belonging. Ousmane Sembène and his sister Faat Sembène had to move their old raggedy shack to the Medina, on Rue 22, right next to the Parc Municipal des Sports (City Sports Complex). As we said earlier, the image of this "portable" makeshift shelter was indelibly imprinted in his memory: "The shack leaned toward the exterior and was upheld by three small beams firmly shoved into the sand; the bottom boards, all worn out, had been patched with zinc plates; the sun had tarnished the red tinge. . . ."[9] According to Maurice Fall, Sembène left for Marseilles from this old itinerant shack located in the Medina.

In addition to the frustrations resulting from France's disgraceful attitude, Sembène was deeply disturbed by the real estate activities of his own family, as he saw in them a blatant injustice. His œuvre is resonant with allusions to these shady family business deals, as in the following dialogue between Oumar Faye and his father in *O pays, mon beau peuple!*:

—THE FATHER: As you know, your grandmother died, may God have mercy upon her and take her under His protection. . . . You were entitled to inherit the house by virtue of your maternal line of descent, but I have leased it for 30 years.

—OUMAR: Nobody told me anything about it beforehand. . . . How can you take possession of something that is not yours, and without letting me know about it in the first place?[10]

The excruciating feeling of having been dissociated from a part of his own self can also be found in *Xala* (1973). This movie tells the story of El Hadji Abdou Kader Bèye, a powerful Muslim businessman who suddenly "turns" impotent on the night of his third marriage. Suspecting a bad spell cast on him by his enemies, he seeks the advice of traditional healers, the marabouts, but their "prescriptions" are of little help. While he is agonizing over his sexual impotence, his business activities slacken, and he eventually loses all his business deals and partners. One day, a beggar comes to the dejected businessman's door. It is the same beggar who has been haunting his office building for several years. The beggar is accompanied by other grim-looking beggars who wreak havoc on the villa. The beggar reveals to El Hadji that he is the one who cursed him with the *xala,* the evil spell, because years before El Hadji had ruined his life. The only way to get rid of the curse is for all the beggars to spit twice upon him while he stands naked. Desperate for an end to his plight, El Hadji agrees. As he endures this humiliation, the police, fearing a riot, surround the house, ready to intervene with guns, bludgeons, and other security paraphernalia.

In *Xala,* the land issue is at the heart of the climactic standoff between El Hadji Abdou Kader Bèye and the leader of the beggars. The latter sums it up very well: "Our story goes way back in the past, it was before your marriage to this woman here. You don't remember it? I knew you wouldn't! What I'm right now [a blind man and a beggar], it's all your fault . . . do you remember selling a big plot of land located in Diéko and that belonged to our clan? With the complicity of people in higher places, you falsified the clan names, *you* expropriated us."[11] Diéko, the place mentioned here, refers to one of the land plots allocated to the Lebu in 1927 through an administrative order, upon the urgings of Blaise Diagne. According to Assane Sylla, each of these plots had an area of 4,300 sq. ft. To come back from the war and find himself compelled to vacate the place where he spent his youth and was grounded in a stabilizing family environment must have been quite frustrating for Sembène. The "homecoming" was, so to speak, spoiled by this downside. However, more than just family decisions, the transfer of Lebu lands was obviously in line with the logic of colonialism and showed the extent to which the administration kept an entire community under increasing pressure. For the Lebus, whose history is punctuated by migrations and struggles to maintain their independence, the fact that they were hard pressed to give over their lands to Lebanese and French traders was indeed a harbinger of dark days ahead and symptomatic of a deeper alienation.

In addition to this internal exile, Sembène saw in Dakar a federal capital fidgeting around "like a thoroughbred caught in a circle of fire," to borrow Cheikh Hamidou Kane's graphic formulation. In spite of the air raids, Dakar could pride itself on having significantly participated in the war effort. The city was thus in a good position to play a pivotal role in the new relationships between France and its West African colonies. This problematic return and the attendant unsettling experiences in a new postwar context led Sembène to dramatic resolutions. He lost all interest in African spirituality and severed all ties with his brothers from the Layène sect, who kept congregating at Mor Seyni's. After he returned from the war, "Ousmane didn't pray anymore," according to Maurice Fall. Was it already the death of God in his heart or a mere spiritual crisis? Was it during the long walks in the Niger desert, when Death was looming large over every sand-swept dune, that this former member of the Layène brotherhood started to feel weary and pissed off, not unlike Sounkaré, another of his characters who would be plagued by spiritual doubt?[12] Sembène's mind may have been abuzz with reflections on human suffering and the deafening silence of God. He may have, like old Sounkaré, set out on a soul-searching mental journey: "Lord . . . Oh Lord who loves me, I am alone on the only road I know. Having suffered as much as I have, I am still at the beginning of suffering. . . . Lord, what are You doing for me? You do not prevent the wicked from doing as they will, nor the good from being crushed beneath the weight of their misery, and by Your commandments You stay the arm of the just man when he would lift it to repair the evil. Do You really exist, or are You just an image? I don't see that You show Yourself anywhere."[13]

Let us not forget that in Casamance, and long before the Layène experience, Ousmane Sembène had also learned from his Mandingo marabouts "to live in the present and to leave tomorrow in the hands of God," with the reassuring certainty that "he would live again after death."[14] But there was another crucial factor for Sembène, namely the role of religious leaders, especially Seydou Nourou Tall, during the war and in their instrumentation by the French who pressed them into service to placate the outraged people of Dakar after the Thiaroye massacre. They certainly used their religious authority to calm things down, but how could someone like Sembène stop thinking about the racial humiliations experienced at the Camp des Mamelles? Sembène could not accept it and his attitude was rather uncompromising, as he once told Carrie Moore: "When I was in the army there were always problems with the whites; I protested and, if I remember alright, I even wrote a letter to Lamine Guèye."[15] From this heady mix of spiritual doubts and social frustrations would emerge a cry, that of Fakeïta in his Bamako prison cell: "[If] God is just, how can He let men be treated so?"[16] But it was another prisoner, the docker Diaw Falla, who expressed unambiguously the break-up between Sembène and religion, no doubt due to the trauma of war: "I had no business with God. . . . Why turn to Him when it is men who are hurting you?"[17] There is a fact worthy of mention here: as in Camus' *The Stranger*, the rejection of God is proclaimed from a prison cell by a man sentenced to death. But from now on, there was another question that kept nagging at Sembène: where will it lead him to, this discovery of a manmade world without transcendence?

10

The Moment of Truth

Even though a number of economic, social, and administrative reforms were initiated at the Brazzaville Conference, on the political level no commitment was made to shake things up. As Xavier Yacono rightly points out, "in the beginning of 1944, the word 'decolonization' sounded dead in French ears, as the ideal of one day turning a French African into an African French remained much valued."[1] Already in 1945 the expression *Union Française* (French Union) started to gain currency, and on July 14 of the same year, the Conseil National de la Résistance (National Council of Resistance) issued a statement during the Etats généraux de la Renaissance française (General States of Reconstruction in France): "We recommend that in the Constitution, overseas territories have a representation equal to a fifth of mainland France, given the fact that former colonies are already represented."[2] In other words, the 40 million Frenchmen represented much more than the 70 million colonized. When, in 1946, French citizenship would be granted to all, the political ramifications of such a landmark decision must be seen in light of this. The bill, known as the *loi Lamine Guèye* (Lamine Guèye Bill), was primarily meant to further assimilationist ends. Sembène, it will be remembered, already enjoyed this French citizenship to which he was entitled by birthright—and it was one of the reasons he fought the war under the French flag.

Sembène regularly read *Le Jeune Sénégal,* a daily newspaper edited by the staunch anticolonialist Pape Guèye Sarr, who was dismissed from the administration for his vitriolic critiques of colonialism. According to Maurice Fall, it was then that Sembène started to become politicized and to reflect on the assimilationist policies advocated by Lamine Guèye, then representing, in the French Parliament, the interests of his constituents from the Four Communes (Dakar, Rufisque, Gorée, and Saint-Louis). Léopold Sédar Senghor, Lamine Guèye's heir apparent, claimed to speak on behalf of both Senegal and Mauritania. The two men were members of the Bloc Africain (African Bloc), a political movement that was hugely popular before it was incorporated, in 1946, into the Senegalese chapter of SFIO headed by the same Lamine Guèye.[3] In spite of minor tactical disagreements, Guèye and Senghor had a common vision for Senegal: French citizenship for all. This desire to remain within the fold of France partly accounted for their conspicuous absence from the Bamako meeting in October 1946, where Apithy (from Dahomey, today Benin), Fily Dabo Cissoko (from French Sudan, today Mali), and Houphouët-Boigny (Ivory Coast) expected Lamine Guèye and Léopold Sédar Senghor to show up and take part in the discussions that would result in the creation of the Rassemblement Démocratique Africain (African Democratic Alliance). RDA was a federation of African parties but had ties with PCF (French Communist Party)—and this was misconstrued as a lingering attachment to France by numerous African political parties, which consequently refused to join the umbrella organization. On May 8, 1950, RDA finally broke up with PCF and drew closer to the Union Démocratique et Socialiste de la Résistance (Socialist and Democratic Union of the Resistance), with François Mitterrand acting as a go-between. With the privilege of hindsight, Sembène's take on the period is quite elucidating: "I think there were two world-shattering events that radically changed Africa's relationship with Europe, but Africans failed to capitalize on them: during World War I, the first generation of Senegalese senior officials, who were schooled in French, fought for their rights as French citizens and never envisaged independence—after all, they had been 'assimilated.' Civil rights claims took precedence over nationalist ones. During World War II, these same Senegalese senior officials kept clamoring for citizenship. Senegal in general, and the inhabitants of the Four Communes in particular, acted in a way that was to prove detrimental to the entire African continent."[4]

On this issue, Sembène was no longer deceiving himself: he knew that French citizenship did not mean anything for an African worker. Even in the Four Communes, Blacks were experiencing racial segregation. In the movie *Camp de Thiaroye,* chief sergeant Diatta, after being tossed from the cafeteria-cum-bordello Le Coq Hardi, under the pretext that he was a "jig," blurts out in anger: "And yet we, Africans, were the ones who booted the Germans out of France!" To which the bar owner, an old French woman, simply replies: "Kiss my ass!"[5] Bara Diouf gives a good description of the atmosphere prevailing in the Plateau at the time: "The group we formed had lived and grown up in a world made up of frustrations, social perversions and brutal shocks. . . . Differences between Blacks and whites were exacerbated, and this resulted in a mutual hatred that was played out every night during epic brawls in the bars and cafés on Rue Raffenel, Rue Ponty, and Rue Grammont."[6] "Cultural universes," adds Bara Diouf, "were as distant from each other as 'planets many light years away from each other.'"[7]

Not surprisingly, Ousmane Sembène often derided Blacks who bragged about their so-called citizenship—it must be pointed out, however, that Sembène himself enjoyed this status, which he would not give up until 1960, when he decided to return to Senegal. Thus in the movie *Guelwaar* (1993), there is a sequence in which Barthélémy is flaunting his French passport in the face of the police officer Gora, who jokingly tells him that he must then seek the help of his embassy if he wants to find the corpse of his deceased father. "Citizenship" was also treated in a parodic vein by Ferdinand Oyono in his novel *Une vie de boy.* On his deathbed in Spanish Guinea (today Equatorial Guinea), Toundi the house boy asks himself: "What are we then, we Africans who are called Frenchmen?"[8] Toundi, like Sembène, came to the bitter realization that there were, as Césaire famously put it, "Frenchmen who were *entirely a part* of the nation" and "Frenchmen who were *entirely apart* from the nation."

Ousmane Sembène was in a good position to experience firsthand what he regarded as the criminal indifference of the elite, and he understood this very early: "We'll never be Europeans or Arabs, never ever. We are and will always remain Africans." According to him, the only assimilationist end worth pursuing would have been to put the Black worker and his French colleague on an equal footing. In point of fact, the Senegalese working class chose to focus on this issue as soon as World War II was over. This acute awareness of themselves as a political force should not come as a surprise, since African workers were the most affected by the war. Ousmane Sembène would later describe their precarious conditions: "The days passed and the nights passed. There was no news, except what every passing hour brought to every home, and that was always the same: the foodstuffs were gone, the meager savings eaten up, and there was no money in the house."[9]

While colonial administration and its "policy makers" were busy "imagining" the future of Africa, the labor world was closing its ranks and reorganizing itself. The leaders of the trade union movement were educated and strongly represented in the administration. Affiliated with the Confédération Générale du Travail (General Confederation of Labor), the unions did not fail to discern the limitations of assimilationist rhetoric. For them African workers had to fight primarily to improve their hard lot. They also knew that theirs was a class struggle. The tone was set in January 1946, when employees in the commerce, industry, and banking sectors (EMCIBA) went on strike, crippling the latter for two weeks. Then the movement spread to other occupational groups, in reaction to the repressive measures adopted by the authorities. More than 2,800 dockers working in the Dakar harbor and the union of metal workers joined the EMCIBA strikers. They created the Union des Syndicats Confédérés (Confederation of Trade Unions), headed by a well-known figure in the labor movement, an *évolué* named Lamine Diallo—who also had close ties with Lamine Guèye.[10] This Confederation also included the union of construction workers, of which Sembène was a member.

Ousmane Sembène lived intensely these troubled hours of 1946: every afternoon he would attend the meetings held at the Pathé Diop Arena, in the vicinity of the Crédit Foncier neighborhood. Other political gatherings took place in Mboth, in the square that used to be opposite the current police station on Rue de Thiong. The speakers, most of whom were senior officials in the administration, voiced the workers' concerns and enumerated their grievances, one by one. This union discourse sharply contrasted with that of the political leaders, who were so obsessed with the issue of citizenship. The workers were more radical and, accordingly, pressed for a radical change in power relationships. Sembène would be deeply marked by their commitment. Concerning the railroad workers who also went on strike the following year, in 1947, he later wrote in the short "author's note" to *God's Bits of Wood:* "The men and women who, from the tenth of October, 1947, to the nineteenth of March, 1948, took part in this struggle for a better way of life, owe nothing to anyone: neither to any 'civilizing mission' nor to any parliament or parliamentarian. Their example was not in vain. Since then Africa has made progress."[11]

The demands formulated by the strikers were clear, accurate, and well documented, and they wanted to compel the authorities to abide by the sacrosanct principle of "equal work, equal pay," as the Thiès *marcheuses* (female marchers)[12] wrote on their banners in 1947. This entailed, among other things, family allowances, decent retirement pensions, and housing benefits. For them, the point was to champion an alternative "assimilation" whereby their merely formal equality with the French workers would be translated into actual reality. Moreover, it was the first time in French West Africa that unions were staking claims for their involvement in the elaboration of occupational listings. As the 1946 trade union movement gained momentum and drew nearly all occupational groups together in a united front, employers grew alarmed and helpless. The strikers were well aware of their strength, and consequently they threatened to extend the movement to the whole region, that is, French West Africa. From Dakar the strike spread like an oil slick, and soon all the workers in Saint-Louis and the Kaolack peanut harbor became involved.

This was no doubt the first "trade union school" for the young Sembène. He later recalled the extent to which he was struck, at the time, by the loud political overtones of the speeches made by leaders such as Lamine Diallo, of the Union des Syndicats Confédérés, and Pape Jean Kâ of EMCIBA. The success of this popular movement was such that for the first time in the colony's history, the authorities—in this case Governor General Cournarie and Masselot, his adviser on labor legislation—were forced to negotiate with the "autochthons." The strike came to an end in the last days of January 1946. Even viewed from a strictly "professional" standpoint, it laid bare the absurdity of a putative "brotherhood" between French and African workers that guaranteed neither equality nor freedom for the latter. Thus, it was the French West African labor movement, not the political class, which first succeeded in paving the way for a total emancipation of the French colonies in Africa. In their negotiations with the *patronat* (organization of company owners), the Dakar union leaders showed that they had a thorough knowledge of not only the whole system of occupational relations, but also of all its attendant theoretical and ideological subtleties. Jean Kâ, for instance, never missed an opportunity to point out to his interlocutors the racism underlying some of their proposals, as when the latter put on the table ludicrous benefits, arguing that "the standard of living of the African worker can in no way be compared to that of his metropolitan colleague." According to many observers, the movement would have dealt a major blow to colonization itself, had peasants in the countryside joined the urban proletariat.

As a young worker and a recent war veteran, Ousmane Sembène was more involved in this strike than in that of the railroad workers, which lasted from 1947 to 1948 and eventually inspired him to pen down his masterpiece, *God's Bits of Wood*. Sembène's recasting of the events in this novel is unanimously considered the most gripping account of working class struggles in Dakar, Senegal, and French West Africa. By all standards, this narrative is simply a literary gem, for it simultaneously shows the death throes of the old and the birth pains of the new Senegalese society during that transitional period: "When a man came back from a meeting, with bowed head and empty pockets, the first things he saw were always the unfired stove, the useless cooking vessels, the bowls and gourds ranged in a corner, empty. . . . The days were mournful, and the nights were mournful, and the simple mewling of a cat set people trembling."[13] From the depths of this ocean of misery surged a tidal wave of revolt nothing could halt, neither the seizures ordered by the inspectors general nor the harsh police repression. The strikers won on all fronts. To take only one example: monthly salaries in the commerce sector increased from 1,540 to 9,500 francs. But beyond these issues related to labor struggles, France had much more to be worried about. The "grand design" of achieving postwar reconstruction and regaining imperial greatness at the expense of the colonies was seriously jeopardized. The war certainly left the colonies drained of all resources, but it also gave rise to a new consciousness among the impoverished African masses. In such a context, drafting a labor legislation for the colonies without taking this new parameter into account had been a serious political mistake. Indeed, the French colonial empire was coming apart at the seams.

Ousmane Sembène resumed his activities as a construction helper after the war, and like most of his childhood friends, those labor struggles directly addressed his own situation. Soon after his return, he joined the union of construction workers headed by Cheikh Diop, who was a construction site manager for the firm Leblanc et Gerbot, located near the Institut

Pasteur. There he rubbed shoulders with Boubacar Diouf "Rafet," head of the Masonry Department at the Pinet Laprade Vocational School. With the exception of Maurice Fall, all his childhood friends were workers, and most of them construction workers. Ousmane Sembène thus reintegrated a labor world that was undergoing deep changes at the time. The "internationalist" dream of some leaders came up against a specifically cultural dynamic: one could not expect African workers to behave according to standards set for European workers. If there was a lesson Sembène drew from the 1946 events, it was that the 15,000 employees in Dakar who crippled the city's economy did not represent a homogeneous and stable "proletariat," in the ideological sense. By granting family allowances to all, even to the lowest-ranking employees in the administration, the authorities implicitly recognized for the first time that urban African workers formed a complex entity—on whose conditions of production and reproduction they had to keep an eye, if they wanted the "colonial order" to prevail in the end.

However, beyond these new ideas, the 1946 social turmoil also gave Sembène the opportunity to take notice of "legendary figures" such as Aynina Fall and Ibrahima Sarr, heroes of the historic strike of the Dakar-Niger railroad workers in 1947–1948. These two would leave deep imprints in Sembène's memory. Ibrahima Sarr was secretary-general of the Fédération des Cheminots d'AOF (Federation of Railroad Workers in French West Africa), which consisted of four networks: Dakar-Niger, Conakry-Niger, Abidjan-Niger, and Benin-Niger. A very pugnacious man, Sarr surrounded himself with outstanding men such as Karim Sow from the union of postal workers, Ousmane Ngom, Cheikh Ndiaye "Teuss-Teuss," and Abdoulaye Bâ. Sembène was impressed with Ibrahima Sarr's moral rectitude. Undaunted by the threats he received from colonial authorities, he rejected the bribe made by Barthes, then High Commissioner of the colony. To the latter, who offered him, in the presence of a great marabout, four million francs, a villa, and a promotion in the metropolitan context, Sarr simply replied: "I'd rather eat stones than accept your offer."[14] There is no doubt that Sembène knew about the episode, for he recreated the same situation in *God's Bits of Wood*. Here is how he describes the confrontation between Doudou, lathe operator and secretary of the federation of railroad workers, and Isnard, the French foreman and manager of the state-owned railroad company: "Isnard's hand was resting on Doudou's shoulder again, and his fingers were tapping gently against the collarbone, but Doudou still said nothing. . . . 'Ah,' Isnard said hastily, 'you almost made me forget the most important thing. Monsieur

Dejean told me that I could put three million francs at your disposition right away. It's not a bribe. . . . It's just an advance.' . . . 'Three million francs is a lot of money for a Negro lathe operator,' Doudou said, 'but even three million francs won't make me white. I would rather have the ten minutes for tea and remain a Negro.'"[15]

As for Aynina Fall, he was always brimming with tremendous energy. Sembène admired his determination and that uncanny ability to always bounce back from his setbacks. Aynina Fall worked at the train station in Dakar, his native city, and chaired the city's committee, of which Djigo Bakari, from Niger, was the secretary-general. According to all those who knew him, Aynina was a man who stood firmly by his principles, and his militancy was truly exceptional. A great orator, his political courage and unswerving sense of honor fascinated Sembène. Aynina Fall formed an excellent pair with Ibrahima Sarr, the other legend in the militant lore of the French West African labor movement.[16] Sembène drew heavily on Ibrahima Sarr's personality traits for the characterization of Ibrahima Bakayoko, the mastermind behind the railroad workers' strike in *God's Bits of Wood,* but it was Aynina who provided the life force needed to sustain the actual historical movement. Fall's deeds are enshrined in the collective memory of Senegal through a popular song in which he is compared to Lat-Dior Ngoné Latir, who opposed the annexation of Kayor during the construction of the Thiès-Saint-Louis railroad line. Léopold Sédar Senghor also celebrated his memory in the poem "Elegy to Aynina Fall."[17]

That these events—and the men who played key roles in them—had a huge impact on Sembène's personal trajectory cannot be denied, judging from the traces they left in his artistic imagination. However, in 1946 there was no indication that Sembène was keenly aware of the implications behind these events. In this respect, Maurice Fall's statement is quite elucidating: "When Ousmane left for Marseilles in 1946, nothing indicated that he would become a writer and a filmmaker; I don't know what happened in Marseilles but it all started from there."[18] Sembène himself could not—or did not want to?—explain this unexpected turn. "It's only now," he calmly observed once to me, "that I can analyze what happened; before I was like everybody, I took events for granted and didn't reflect on them." And he adds, giving a glimpse of his treasured writerly ego: "People of my generation lived in the same environment as me, but we didn't all follow the same path. It's like the land and the trees: there is only one land, but you have countless tree varieties, although they all draw off their sap from the same land."[19] In other words, Sembène the introvert, the sensitive man whom life dealt, so to speak, many blows, had been more influenced than others by the postwar social movement. But such an observation is of little help to someone who wants to grasp Sembène's personality and crack the hard nut of his mysterious singularity.

What then was the pivotal event that changed his life and turned him, from 1946 on, into such a solitary man? One could perhaps mention, in one fell swoop, the divorce of his parents during his early childhood; his rebellious spirit; the war; his labor experience; and also the educational failures out of which grew his insatiable desire to learn. His status as a second-class citizen may have caused frustrations and made him wary of human beings. As his fictional mouthpiece, Diaw Falla, says to his friend Paul Sonko in *Black Docker*: "When they're cold, they don't bite, you know. It's the living you should be afraid of, not the dead."[20] There is another question worth asking: what incited Sembène to leave? Even today it is hard to find the right answer to this enigma. The famous "Parisian mirages" may well have lured him into their deceptive fantasy-worlds, but the prime motives behind his decision to leave remain somewhat vague. Ousmane Sembène felt no doubt constrained by his surroundings. According to Maurice Fall, it is also possible that he already had a clear-cut, but secret, plan in his head when he left for France. One thing, however, can be accepted as certain: the books and movies of his errant teenage years did carry much weight in his decision making: "I have learned a language which is not my own. At school, they told me about the goodness of a city and when I came to this country, to live, I had to work," said Diaw Falla in his final letter.[21] And like Diouana, the main protagonist in "La noire de . . . ," Sembène "wanted to see France and come back from this country that everybody was glorifying, saying how beautiful, wealthy, and pleasant to live in it was! One could make a fortune there."[22] Frantz Fanon pointedly described this fascination of the colonized for Europe: "There is a kind of magic vault of distance, and the man who is leaving next week for France creates round himself a magic circle in which the words *Paris, Marseilles, Sorbonne, Pigalle* become the keys to the vault. He leaves for the pier, and the amputation of his being diminishes as the silhouette of his ship grows clearer."[23]

Maurice Fall remembers one unforgettable September night, in 1946, on the eve of his friend's departure for Marseilles. They met in the makeshift shack Ousmane shared with his sister Faat Sembène, in the Medina. The two young men had a brief conversation:

"Ousmane, why do you want to leave this country and go to France? You'll be bored to death there, you don't know anybody, you'll end up a bum."

"I won't stay idle, I may even resume my studies."

"Resume your studies! At your age, you want to go back to the classroom!"

Maurice Fall offered me his retrospective comments on the aftermath of this meeting: "As usual, Ousmane withdrew into complete silence. I knew him well: the fact that he didn't answer me any further meant his decision was irrevocable."[24]

The next morning, Ousmane Sembène embarked on a journey to Marseilles—as a stowaway—aboard the *Pasteur,* a commercial ship that was also used to repatriate the African soldiers who fought on various European fronts during World War II. Like Diouana, the heroine of the short story "Black Girl" aboard *l'Ancerville,* here was Ousmane Sembène on his way to the south of France, where he hoped to shape his own destiny: "Eight days at sea . . . Water all around you, in the front, in the back, to starboard, to port . . . nothing but a broad liquid expanse, and the sky overhead."[25]

PART FOUR

THE MAKING OF A MILITANT-ARTIST

Victor Gagnaire and Ousmane Sembène in Marseille, circa 1950.
Photo courtesy of Ousmane Sembène.

Love cares no more about caste
Than about race—neither does Sleep fret about a pallet.
I went in search of Love,
And I lost my way. . . .

—Ousmane Sembène, *O pays, mon beau peuple!*

11

"The Village"

"Once upon a time, there was a king who ruled over a small territory, in the south of what would later become France. This dates back to a distant and forgotten past, twenty-six centuries ago, to be accurate."[1] Thus began an article written by Michel Richard, the first in a special issue that the magazine *Le Point* devoted to Marseilles, to celebrate the city's 2,600 years of existence. Michel Richard reminds us that the oldest French city is "at heart a rebellious city, and this trait still remains, after all.... A city with the pride of a peacock, with its own accent and its own pace; the only thing that matters to her is, in the final analysis, her soul as a unique community."[2] Laurent Theis also highlights some other distinctive features of the Phocean city: "More Greek than Roman, contiguous with Provence, ill-fatedly tacked to France and often ill-at-ease within the kingdom, more Catholic by allegiance than Christian by temperament, prematurely republican and belatedly royalist, laboring hard to accommodate modern democracy, at once

cosmopolitan and identity-sensitive, Marseilles never seems to be truer to itself than when it resists, and such is always the case when, in a loving embrace, it welcomes the sea and its legion of merchant ships."[3]

"What I like most, over and above anything else in the world, are cities cut through by waterways, like Ziguinchor, Dakar, Paris or Marseilles. Water is for me a fundamental element. . . . It's hard for me to explain why, it's a kind of gut-feeling."[4] These statements can help us better understand, among other matters, why Ousmane Sembène immediately fell in love with Marseilles, this Mediterranean crossroads. The harbor, the first in France, went through "a complete curing as early as the 17th century and subsequently increased its shippability, already looking far out in the distance":[5] the Levant, the West Indies, West Africa, the East Indies, and even America. All these worlds opened up by the sea have enriched Massalia[6] and turned it into this fabled city of encounters between various peoples. Legend has it that Marseilles owes its very creation to the ocean and seafaring: "Around 600 BC, Phoceans (Greeks from Asia Minor) aboard a handful of galleys and seeking ways of expanding their trade activities, eventually landed on the Lakydon creek, where is today located the Vieux Port."[7] Marseilles, the "111-neighborhood-city," as Michel Flacon calls it, is the second French city and by far the most cosmopolitan of all, on account of the successive migratory waves that have punctuated its history: Poles, Italians, Armenians, North Africans, Sub-Saharan Africans, Asians, Pieds-Noirs,[8] and Comorians. In 1913, the harbor's activities were such (10,000,000 freight tons and 600,000 passengers) that Jean Louis Parisis enthused: "Judging from the statistics and the ads in the *Messageries Maritimes* . . . one is entitled to wonder whether the world hasn't simply become an extension of Marseilles!"[9]

Marseilles is also known for giving witty—yet far from funny—winks to history. Thus in 1922, the mayor Siméon Flaissières launched a campaign to convince public opinion that immigration posed serious threats to the city—and the nation at large. Mayor Flaissières was a very outspoken man, he did not go for the sugar-coated rhetoric of most French politicians: "Exceptional measures are needed in times like this, and the population of Marseilles strongly urges the government to prohibit the entry, through French harbors, of these immigrants and that it repatriate, without further delay, these beggarly human herds that are endangering the whole nation."[10] Like most port cities at a time when rivers and oceans were the only communication routes linking various parts of the world, Marseilles served for a long time as a bridge between France and its colonial possessions, even after the advent of civil aviation. In this last respect, Marseilles was, for everyone in search of freedom, wealth, or simply their deeper selves, the gateway to distant places holding out the promise of a fresh start in life. If Paris was, back then, the "natural" destination for most African intellectuals, Marseilles by contrast attracted seafarers, sailors, dock workers, and of course unemployed persons—most of whom entered France illegally. The city even became the hub of the colonial migrant community: according to a 1926 census report, out of the 2,580 Africans and Malagasies in France, more than a third lived in Marseilles, and among these there were 14 students and 800 sailors.[11] Of course, these figures do not take into account illegal immigrants, who are always, as is well known, the invisible majority. In this multicultural context, Ousmane Sembène, the former construction helper and *gobi*[12] in the colonial infantry, felt in his natural element—and he would easily fit into it, as we shall see.

Owing to its geographical location, the city was dragged into the war as early as 1939, but there would be no attempt to take full control of it until June 17, 1940: on that night, Mussolini's forces launched a raid against the neighborhoods around the harbor. The attack lasted only one hour, but left 143 dead and nearly as many wounded. According to Roger Duchêne and Jean Contrucci, up to November 1942, following the Allied invasion of North Africa, Marseilles was the life and soul of the Zone Sud (Southern Zone), free from any German occupation. A rallying point for Jews fleeing Nazi persecutions, Marseilles also attracted those who volunteered to join the French Resistance, as well as hundreds of writers and artists who wanted to leave the occupied areas or were simply anxious to escape Vichy censorship.[13] On January 16, 1943, the Germans dynamited the area located between the Vieux Port and Rue Caisserie, causing it to be completely vacated. Two thousand homes were destroyed, and there were 20,000 internally displaced, including 780 Jews who were quickly sent to Auschwitz. From this date on, and up until its liberation by the Allied troops in May 1944, every day the city had to bear the brunt of German occupation and vicious terrorist attacks perpetrated by Vichy collaborators. But Marseilles was also a site of resistance in which various movements had invested: CGT, which had to go underground after Pétain outlawed trade unions; MOI (Immigrant Labor Power) which had ties with the French Communist Party; and the Organization of Armed Resistance (ORA). It is estimated that 1,500 natives of Marseilles, fighting in the Resistance, were killed in action. As should be expected, Hitler's defeat gave rise to a huge victory celebration. According to General Monsabert, there were no words to describe this popular fervor, this "*Canebière* lined with armored tanks, [these] road intersections swarming with cannons, quays in the Vieux Port abuzz with the parades of Allied troops, colonial soldiers and *goumiers*."[14]

In September 1946, Ousmane Sembène had thus come to a city that was trying to shake off the traumatic memory of four years of humiliations and deprivations: "I arrived after the war, after countless tribulations in my life; many of my companions had passed away and myself I had always lived with the shadow of death cast over my head."[15] Postwar reconstruction was fully underway in Marseilles, and the city was busy recovering from its wounds while preparing for the future. After Libération, thousands of migrants from the colonies flocked to Marseilles, along with repatriated French nationals—at least for a time. In the early '50s, Ousmane Sembène was a well-known figure in the circles of African immigrants. He was the "black docker" from Senegal envisioning a better world and inciting his fellow sufferers to revolt against their hard lot. His years in Marseilles are written all over the fiery pages of "Lettres de France" ("Letters from France," one of the short stories in the collection *Voltaïque*) and *Black Docker,* pages burning with desires, with the heady feeling of a newly gained knowledge, the agonies of a divided self, the vicissitudes of his quest for the Other; but they were also burning with conflict and love. Through his first novel, inspired by his personal experience as a docker in Marseilles, Ousmane Sembène wanted to draw the attention of public authorities to the plight of Black workers in France—and he had specifically in mind the African representatives in Paris.

After the war, explains a former labor leader, when a new immigrant arrived, "the first thing he did was to go in search of his countrymen, of people who came from the same community."[16] Marseilles was then a highly segregated city, although this segregation proceeded along class, not racial, lines; and there was a huge gap between the affluent people of the Prado and the lumpen proletariat living in "the little Harlem of Marseilles."[17] Here is how Sembène describes the former in *Black Docker:* "There is no doubt that the most prestigious part of Marseilles is the Prado. The main thoroughfare is flanked by two symmetrical banks, planted with four rows of trees. The houses with ivy- and honeysuckle-covered walls try to outdo each other in elegance. The people who live in them are the flower of the city."[18] In spite of the inescapability of death as the common fate of all mortals, even in the graveyard the novel's narrator registers some signs of these class inequalities: "monuments adorned with inert angels. Flowers thrived around the mausoleums."[19] In contrast to this dazzling world of the rich, the narrator sees a "procession of Blacks. It was very simple, no wreaths, no trappings. . . . The graves became smaller and less elaborate . . . the wilting yellow grass drooped over the daisies."[20] Ousmane Sembène found a room in "Little Harlem," which he also dubbed "The Village," a poverty-stricken area whose intersecting streets and churches he vividly captured in this detailed description:

> As you walk down the main road, the rue des Dominicaines, and enter the little Harlem of Marseilles, you will see the parish church of Saint-Théodore to your left. Many people still call it by the name given to it by the Franciscan monks: the church of the Récollet fathers. A few yards away is an intersection where the rue des Petites-Maries leading to the station crosses the rue des Dominicaines which continues down to the boulevard d'Athènes. The rue des Baignoires runs at right angles to the other two, making a triangle around a single building which forms the heart of the district.[21]

Sembène had internalized the "geography" of this urban space, and its symbolic dimension was not lost on him. Most Senegalese people lived in the dingy boardinghouses around the Rue du Baignoir, Rue des Dominicaines, and Rue des Petites-Maries, a commercial area where sundry immigrant trades were flourishing. Although colonials traditionally resided in Belsunce, most of the seamen and dockers lived in the vicinity of the harbor, in La Joliette and Le Panier, the two neighborhoods where employment and welfare agencies were located, as well as some charity organizations.

Upon his arrival in Marseilles, Ousmane Sembène initially settled in Belsunce, before moving, a couple of years later, to a rented room in the neighborhood of l'Opéra, on Rue Sylvabelle. After Thiédem and the Medina in Dakar, here he was again, an immigrant settled in "The Village" of Marseilles—as if he were doomed to always end up living with "the wretched of the earth." In the Vieux Quartier (Old Neighborhood), where the Black population, following the two world wars, had significantly increased, Sembène was appalled by the "squalid, narrow, dead-end streets."[22] Belsunce and its shabby rooms for rent, its cheap food joints with their more than loose hygiene standards, its cafés, restaurants and bars . . . Belsunce where tensions between immigrants were sometimes played out in bloody fights involving the gangs of the two roughnecks, Babou Senghor the Senegalese giant and Kader the Moroccan. In the Rue des Dominicaines, the Boulevard des Dames or the Cours Belsunce, the cellars of the taverns run by French or Italian traders often served as meeting or game rooms, as hiring places and even rings for improvised boxing matches.[23] Ousmane Sembène soon attracted attention through his involvement in various community organizations—it was even rumored that at some point the Renseignements Généraux, the French secret service, inquired into his activities.[24] And yet at the time, the reasons behind his activism had little to do with politics and were more tied to his practical humanism, which was in turn grounded in his firsthand experience with the downtrodden.

It will be remembered that in the 1920s, Siméon Flaissières, then mayor of Marseilles, had vowed to drive back all illegal immigrants from the colonies. However, Africans were not the only Blacks in Marseilles, there were also many African Americans, as can be seen in Claude McKay's *Banjo,* in which the Jamaica-born writer paints a vivid picture of this Black presence in the Phocean city.[25] Further, the African population of Marseilles was still relatively small, compared to that of migrant communities from Italy and other parts of Europe. But from 1946 on, migratory waves from the colonies increased significantly, and "Black people poured in from all sides, drawn by the vicissitudes of seafaring and life in general."[26] Among the inhabitants of this Village, this "little Africa in the south of France," many were former seamen and had sailed all the oceans on the planet. According to available figures, the bulk of these seasoned sailors was made up by the Sarakoles. Then came, in decreasing order, Joolas, Mandingos, and the "aristocracy" of African seamen, the Wolofs, who mostly came from the Four Communes. By virtue of their French citizenship, these latter had received, like Sembène, some basic training in the French school system. The African colony also included a small portion of Guineans, the Susus, who served as *boys,* waiters or line cooks. In *Black Docker,* Sembène did not fail to portray, with subtle sociological indications, this motley community of African immigrants:

> There were Sarakoles, the most numerous, for whom life would not be worth living if they could not go to sea. . . . The Susus were wily, cunning and timorous, while the Malinkes[27] were calm and ponderous. The Tukulors, descendants of the conqueror El Hadji Omar, were very dignified in their movements. The [Manjaks][28] and the [Joolas] were nicknamed "the African Bretons" because of their love of wine. The warrior Bambara, without whom the bravery of the African soldier would not be legendary . . . a few Dahomeens, calm and thoughtful, Martiniquans, Moors . . .[29]

This migrant community, quite diverse in its origins but united in misery, was concentrated in the 1er arrondissement (First District) and had its social club on Rue Puvis de Chavannes. Out of the 4,000 people who formed that community in the '50s, only 350 were gainfully employed. For the overwhelming majority, Marseilles was akin to a distant island onto which the tidal waves of circumstance had hurled them like shipwrecked sailors: "Retired navy soldiers, war veterans or seamen without a ship since the advent of modernization and the downsizing of flotillas . . . all rejected a free repatriation to their home countries, a training in various construction trades. . . ."[30] The resulting high unemployment rate was also due to the shift to diesel engines in sea transportation, sounding the death knell of coal-trimming, a job slot that was mainly filled by Africans. Moreover, on account of their lack of professional qualifications and their low proficiency in French, these African seamen could not work on boat engines. To make matters even worse, the destruction of the French flotilla during the war and the need to enable demobilized French sailors to find jobs back on their own turf implied that the "natives" could in no way compete with these "born and bred" Frenchmen—who were often better trained to staff these positions, in any case. A tiny fraction of this disadvantaged workforce had to make do with small and precarious jobs in the shipyards. Thus, it was even hard to find a job as a docker, since it provided a modicum of financial security.

In light of all these factors, one can see how fortunate Sembène was to be hired as a docker. Through this activity, he gained acquaintance with, among others, Madess Fara, a sailor from Bissau-Guinea; the Malian Madigou Diawara, head of the Association des Africains de Marseille (African Association of Marseilles); and Mamadou Kanté from Guinea. Among the Senegalese, there were Ibrahima Diallo, also known as "Bouki,"[31] Idrissa Diop, a 7-foot-tall docker and boxer; and his co-workers Hamat Diop and Victor Sané. The Senegalese bar, on Rue Magenta, was run by a Wolof popularly known as Vieux Cheikh Diop. However, of all these acquaintances, the legendary Babou Senghor is the one who deserves special mention here. As a unit leader in the Quai de la Joliette, he is said to have facilitated the hiring of Sembène. A multifaceted fellow who arrived in Marseilles one year before Sembène, Babou Senghor was also active in the African nationalist movement. He had been a combatant in General de Gaulle's Forces Françaises Libres (Armed Forces of Free France) and was eventually awarded the Croix de Guerre (Military Cross) and the Médaille Coloniale (Colonial

Medal). Thanks to his prodigious physical strength, he reigned over the rings of Marseilles's Black section and terrorized bar fighters in such places as the Nice Bar, the Bar de la coloniale, and the François. But while Sembène had already joined the CGT-affiliated Union of Dockers, Babou Senghor had earned himself a bad reputation as a scab: it was a case of the war hero turned labor mercenary.

Life in Marseilles was anything but easy for Sembène. "I didn't live like a student," he says in retrospect. On this side of the Mediterranean, the erstwhile construction helper linked up again with his people, "men and women scantily dressed who had barely enough to live on and who were quite conspicuous on the sick lists of welfare agencies." An "educated" person and a French "citizen," Ousmane Sembène was then a man with high ambitions and great existential projects. He had a broader perspective than most of his fellow sufferers and was more sensitive to certain changes in French society. In a sense, he was both inside and outside a world that had a tremendous influence on his major life choices. Once he settled in the Village, it did not take him too long to realize that his people were stuck deep down in the bottomless pit of ignorance, and because of this they would never be able to rise up the social ladder. These "temporary exiles" had left their distant native countries only to see the high walls of prejudice and xenophobia gradually close in on them, condemning them to pursue a chimera.

At the end of World War I, the toughest and most underpaid jobs in Marseilles were laid aside for African immigrants. They were either greasers or coal heavers shoveling up wheelbarrows and dumping them into ship cargos. As there were few Africans available for these chores, they became very much in demand. As the old Sarakole in *Black Docker* recalls, "at the time [1901] there were only three of us. . . . They would come and beg us to sail with such and such or such and such a company."[32] After the war, technological advances forced immigrants into unemployment. Unlike their European counterparts, these workers were not entitled to any social security benefits and thus had to live from hand to mouth. Too old to find another job, they could not go back home either, where they would still be treated like strangers. Ousmane Sembène's early works faithfully chronicle the daily hardships of these ostracized immigrants; their poverty was the seedbed of public and domestic violence, but it was also the source of physical and moral decay. Michel Libermann, a friend and former comrade of Sembène's during his communist period, recalls that in those days few Africans migrated to Marseilles with the intent of staying definitively in France. Rather, they regarded themselves as seasonal workers with a straightforward plan: hoard up a significant amount of money before heading back home. In the postwar period, this dream of a successful return was crystallized in the "suitcase metaphor." Bougouma Seck, who in 1998 was still the imam of a mosque in Marseilles, also lived through the '50s in a boardinghouse on Rue des Dominicaines. He calculated that in just a couple of years he could fill up his "suitcase" and get back home. Ibrahima Barro, who also worked as a docker in Marseilles during that period, had a similar scheme. Sembène took Barro under his protection when the latter arrived in Marseilles in 1956. A former lighting engineer at the Daniel Sorano National Theater in Dakar, where he lives today in retirement, Barro recalls with nostalgia this much-fabled suitcase: "At the time we often had temporary contracts, but that didn't bother us, our successful return to Africa was foremost in our minds. In the Cours Belsunce, a Polish Jew trader sold a 'suitcase' to every incoming immigrant. The latter had then to make a monthly payment, and the Pole would put aside for him clothes, bikes, shotguns or other items to bring back home."[33]

That suitcase would never fill up, and its owner's dream of going back home would never come true. However, it should be noted that in those days immigrants were less concerned about settling into their new environments or any other form of integration. While looking forward to this hypothetical return, the immigrant bade his time in one of the rented rooms Sembène described in his first novel: "In one corner was an iron bed at the foot of which was a bidet and a washbasin. In the opposite corner was a wardrobe with only half the mirror remaining. Next to it was a table surrounded by a red curtain. On the oilcloth with scorch marks was a dusty oil stove."[34] Immigrants were crammed in each of these tiny rooms, and roommates often were matched according to the criterion of a common place of origin—country, city, or even village. Doubly exiled, they found some solace in nostalgic "remembrance of things past," of the good old days and the happy life they had been leading *back home.*

Ousmane Sembène conjured up images of this half real, half idyllic land of memory in *Black Docker:*

At a distance, the blacks stood chatting in a group outside the Ferréol café, with nothing but an occasional indifferent glance at the scene taking place before them. They spoke the most diverse mixture of languages. All their topics of conversation were related to home, to their wives and families or a hope they nurtured which collapsed the moment the dream became a reality. Sometimes one of them would put his hand in his pocket and bring out a letter he had read over and over again, his eyes wandering over the geometry of the words as if he wanted to absorb every syllable. It came from home and he would report the news to the others. And they would daydream again, about the betrothed or about the animals bought to celebrate an alliance. The only thing they did not forget was their village and their patch of land, for that was something nobody could take away from them.[35]

Sembène's passing allusion to the immigrants' linguistic diversity is worthy of note. In point of fact, there were so many languages that cross-cultural exchanges were always uneasy, and interactions with French people even harder to sustain. In the harbor, Babou Senghor, the strike breaker, was living proof of the French labor movement's failure to enter into an alliance with this teeming mass of Black immigrants. But what did a Parisian worker have in common with a Guinean docker in Marseilles who could not speak French? The very few educated African workers, like Sembène, could at least get involved in labor movements and become members of progressive organizations such as CGT and the PC. Later on, Sembène enlarged his range of militant activities, which would then include the struggle against imperialism—an alignment with the Soviet Union in the context of the Cold War that led to his brief internship in Prague, in October 1958. These experiences broadened the scope of his mind and enabled him to escape the parochialism prevailing in an environment where "ethnic cleavages were as important as social and professional disparities, while the perennial squabbles of French politicians held no interest for Black seamen. The latter would only get organized when hard pressed by hunger, and would join the unions only when they were promised a 'priority boarding' on the next ship."[36] Through his active involvement in labor movements, Sembène had, to a certain extent, secured the best vantage point from which to observe this world of labor where existential pressures stifled any ideal, any longing for a better life. Thus, of his companions in Marseilles, he could have said, like Diaw Falla in *Black Docker*: "They were all at an impasse, they did not know who to turn to. Events had overtaken them, they were groping about in the dark and poverty made them blinder. . . . They did not know what the root of the problem was and they made their demands in a vacuum."[37] Despair led the immigrants to withdraw into themselves, a defense mechanism Sembène also described in "Lettres de France": "Most of the time I'm shut down. . . . There is only one room for the two of us," says the heroine, forced to migrate to Marseilles where, with her old unemployed husband, an occasional cola-nut seller, she lives "in a room that serves as a kitchen, a laundry room and a bathroom. When, in the middle of the night, I have to answer the call of nature, I don't go out. I have a portable urinal. . . . My room is what they call a 'dark room.' . . . The sun never visits it."[38]

The immigrant's isolation and invisibility were so complete that Bernard Worms, the great internationalist militant, confessed that if it were not for his acquaintance with Sembène, he may have never become sensitive to the problems that beset African immigrants. No doubt this gaping void must have aroused in him, as in his friend, a sickening feeling. A loneliness and a "nausea" that is noted in *Black Docker,* and which have some bearing on Diaw Falla's world-weary attitude:

> *One day, he entered a wine cellar in the Rue des Dominicaines. He was filled with disgust. He studied the interior in minute detail. There were several people, either sitting or standing around the barrels serving as tables. They were of both sexes, black and white. The glasses or the bottles were passed from mouth to mouth, from thin lips to thick lips. In a corner, slumped a man as limp as a half-empty sack, his head lolling on to his stomach. Between his spread-eagled legs was a pool of vomit, a mixture of red and green. One of his feet was stained and there were splashes on his jacket. His big toe was poking out of his left shoe. The vile smell of the bar nauseated Diaw, forcing him to leave. This scene destroyed the pleasure of all the beauty he had seen.*[39]

But Sembène did not resign himself to his fate. He was brimming with an energy that could only have sprung from an unwavering faith in the future. He could not, even for a second, imagine himself passively standing by while all around him things were falling apart. Another world was possible, and it behooved him, together with other victims of this unfair system, to fight the status quo and effect some change. "Those foundering creatures," says Diaw Falla after watching that surreal scene in the wine cellar, "are castaways, swept along by the ocean of time. Poor wretches, they cling to the bottle. . . . What about me, what will be my destiny?"[40]

As in Dakar, Ousmane Sembène daily experienced racism in Marseilles, for there too "race mattered" a great deal, as Cornel West would have put it. Yet Sembène always refused to see everything from the perspective of a racially prejudiced man, sensing that race was merely a variable in a more complex equation. As evidenced by *Black Docker, O pays, mon beau peuple!,* and even *God's Bits of Wood*, Sembène never lost sight of the class factor inherent in the immigrant experience. To him, this became all the more obvious when he saw white employers use Africans as scabs to replace striking white workers, and "the latter harbored a deep resentment that would later serve to legitimate colonial oppression and plunder."[41] Many years later, Sembène still claimed solidarity with all those who toil to generate the wealth of a society, and not only with his oppressed African brothers scattered all over the world. Even though this larger class consciousness was already taking shape in colonial Dakar, it was in Marseilles that Sembène's attitude toward the outside world radically changed. But what experiences formed the "stuff" of this legendary docker's life, from which he emerged to become such a prominent writer and filmmaker?

12

The Docker

Ousmane Sembène worked as a docker at the Place de la Joliette, Quay J3, Gate 25. Before that he used to do some stints as a day laborer, but he did not have a professional card. In postwar Marseilles, a docker was always associated with foreignness and poverty. Sembène was then in his prime, performing his herculean tasks to the best of his physical abilities. But five years later, an accident would incapacitate him, forcing Sembène out of the job. Five years spent working like a galley slave to unload ship holds and during which Sembène had to drink deep from the bitter cup of exploitation—but he would also learn, in the process, how to fight against it alongside thousands of other men.

By 1949 the Marseilles harbor, one of the nerve centers of French economy in the aftermath of World War II, was fully rebuilt—it had been severely damaged after countless German air raids. According to many concurring accounts, the important harbor traffic required steady work, night and day, regardless of weather conditions. "At night," writes Alfred Pacini, a retired docker,

> it was as if things were taking place in broad daylight, the ships had all their lights on, their winches at full speed and the crane pulleys bent toward them. . . . Trucks were coming and going, creating an infernal din . . . and there were always thousands of men busy with their work. In 1949 alone, an estimated 6,000 ships entered the Marseilles harbor, which represented more than 10 million tons of goods and 1 million passengers.[1]

Today, container ships have revolutionized maritime cargo handling. At docking, unmanned cranes hoist the packed goods, stored in huge containers, out of the cargo ship and safely place them on the wharf or load them onto trucks. The process is now faster, cleaner, and less hazardous. This new system is so efficient that employment security is the only issue labor organizations have with it.

Things were altogether different in Sembène's time, as most tasks required manual laborers. "A docker's job was tough, extremely tough. Every day we had to carry on our backs more than five hundred tons of goods."[2] According to Emile Bellundy, who, until 1953, also worked as a docker,

> Ships from around the world visited the Marseilles harbor, many coming from Africa, South-East Asia (after the Suez Canal was opened in 1869), America and as far as the Iles de la Sonde.[3] Since many ships had to pass through Marseilles, we sometimes received up to 40 of them on a single day; whereas now [in 1997], it takes less than a day to unload a ship, in our time it took us eight days.[4]

Quay J3, where Sembène was assigned, received mostly ships loaded with fresh fruits and vegetables. Over the years, the harbor would undergo numerous changes, both technical and in terms of its symbolic relationship with the city; these changes would even affect the relations between those who worked in it. Obviously, the harbor is not a mere pass-through area for all kinds of goods; out of its docksides and warehouses, which take up 32 square kilometers, has also evolved a genuine social microcosm where sailors, traders, and dockers interact every day. The harbor is certainly a space fraught with human paradoxes and contradictions, but more crucially, and as Albert Pacini reminds us, it is also an infinite "space of freedom"—and as such it perfectly suited Sembène's personality.

In his investigation report "Marseille, porte du Sud" ("Marseilles: A Gateway to the South"), the journalist and travel writer Albert Londres, who was also a longtime observer closely following the Marseilles harbor's evolution throughout the years, asked this at once simple and crucial question: *what is a docker?* "Of course," he writes, "you will be told: 'It's just someone who loads or unloads ships in harbors.' . . . The docker is that man who, in the docks, hauls up bundles by the score. But who is this man who 'chooses' to become a docker?"[5] Londres wrote his long, in-depth report in 1927, to denounce the appalling conditions in which dockers had to live and work, but even three decades later, those who were labeled *les chiens des quais*[6] could still not even claim a worker status, for a worker is someone who exerts a professional activity learned through training, whether it be construction work, pottery, baking, and so forth. One does not learn to be a docker, "one simply *becomes* a docker. To work as a miner, an ironsmith or an ebony wood carver, means to have a profession. The docker has none. . . . One finds workers among the dockers, and they are precisely unemployed workers. A docker is someone who works hard because there is nothing else to do."[7] If there is any freedom of "choice" for the docker, it only consists in his being free to live and die like a dog.

The term "docker" was coined after the Compagnie des Docks, a shipping trade company, was granted a concession in 1854. Through the monopoly it wielded in Marseilles, the word gained currency and by 1864 it had passed into popular usage. To give a sense of the thousands of hours Sembène spent in ship holds, one need only refer to the opinion of Marseilles-born shipping cognoscenti on how, in those days, the docker was perceived. According to Alfred Pacini,

> a negative image was automatically tagged to him. . . . The docker, he was the pariah, a mere cog in the great machine operated by external evil forces that had imposed the harbor's modernization. This modernization, impelled by people who were not born in Marseilles, raised serious concerns, for a long-established situation was being turned upside down. As an agent of the "enemy," the docker inspired fear. He was both foreign and poor.[8]

In keeping with such xenophobic feelings, the docker was seen as an abnormal being, the type who would "leave his children on the streets, who cares little, if at all, about them, and puts them on the job market as soon as they are out of the cradle. He is an alcoholic propping up the bars in La Joliette and Belsunce, a robber who shamelessly pilfers on the quays and diverts some of the goods for his private use or to sell them again."

In Sembène's docking area, sugar arrived in sacks weighing 330 pounds. Once in the hold, dockers had to hoist them, using a hook or a pallet, onto their backs or, more often, they had to team up in pairs to carry these heavy loads. In the short story "Chaïba," Sembène describes this team effort:

> Chaïba worked as a docker. . . . He was in my unit . . . a good helping hand. Over the hours, shifts, workdays, weeks and months, he became the best teammate I'd ever had. . . . As if we were one person, our thoughts converged whenever we had to handle, roll or lift something. Without exchanging a single word, we simultaneously sighted the best spot where to put down the load.[9]

But as many former dockers have pointed out, including Albert Pacini, the task was physically more than taxing:

> To lift and carry [these loads], you would have had to squat and then get up vertically, using the thigh muscles, not the hips, to straighten yourself. . . . Instead, you bend forward, you take one sack or box and you lift it up while trying to straighten yourself. Then you walk. . . . It breaks your back, it crushes your vertebrae, it hurts, and getting the hang of it doesn't help. A docker suffers from back pains all his life.[10]

In addition to his hands, this back is the docker's only available tool for a physically demanding job. For the former colonial soldier, carrying knapsacks during the long desert marches in Niger must have, then, looked like child's play compared to this literally backbreaking activity. However, the docks were also, especially for Sembène, the setting of countless formative experiences through which men were imbued with a strong sense of dignity, self-esteem, and a willingness to earn respect by doing an impeccable job. As attested by all the former dockers I interviewed, when a ship left the Marseilles harbor, its captain readily enthused over the certainty that there was nothing to worry about, as the stowage of cargoes was flawless. Ship captains, their officers and, broadly speaking, all those involved in shipping activities, admitted that the Marseilles dockers worked efficiently and were among the best in the world.[11]

In addition to the physical effort the docker had to muster, work pace and duration were also stress factors. Ship owners, always anxious to reach the next harbor as quickly as possible, imposed tight, nearly impossible schedules, while enticing dockers to do overtime work. Albert Brachet, a retired docker and currently the legal adviser of the CGT chapter in Marseilles, observes: "The docker was a nobody: he came in the morning, was hired and given a token with a number on it. Then he went down into the hold, and he never knew when he would get out of it. When he was lucky enough to be hired, the docker was often forced to work overtime, and this as soon as he had completed his first regular eight hours."[12] As a "beast of burden,"[13] Ousmane Sembène intimately experienced these long successive hours in the pulses of his muscles and the agony of his vertebrae. Moreover, the weather was another aggravating factor:

> Not only was the work hard, but winter made the workers belligerent. The rain and wind froze their fingers and their ears felt as though they would split open. They kept their jackets on for the first shift. . . . Diaw Falla's nerves were on edge from the combination of exhaustion and debilitation caused by overwork.[14]

All these difficulties were summed up very graphically in a report sent by a labor inspector to his superiors: "A thick cloud of dust pervaded the room. Soon all our clothes were covered with this dust, and it gradually became harder to breathe, due to the lack of air circulation in the space left vacant and to the foulness of the atmosphere. . . . The dockers' faces were smeared with all the dust shored up by the sweat."[15] In like manner, Albert Londres's portrayal of a docker's life in the late 1920s could also apply to the conditions Sembène was living in during the fifties:

> Around 11:30 AM, morning work is over and the dockers file back past the Joliette. They are going to have lunch. What have they done, these men, to smell so bad? As if they had drunk so much cod liver's oil that in the end this oil seeps out through all their pores. . . . Some have been shoveling up coal in wheelbarrows, an awfully hard task, and they have been coughing all this morning; some others are covered from head to toe in red, they are the ones who carry wheat sacks. It's bad, this wheat powder, especially in the holds. . . . Some continually spit on account of the saltpeter; some others cry: too much exposure to sulphur.[16]

Until 1955, in most of the harbor's warehouses there were no bathrooms, no refectories, no locker rooms, no drinking water for the dockers. Most were thus walking the tightrope between physical exhaustion and mental deterioration.

It hardly needs saying that Sembène was deeply marked by this period of his life. "In the place de la Joliette," he later wrote,

> there was a human tide. The quayside workers poured on to the esplanade by tram, bus and on foot. . . . The uncertainty of work inflamed the abcess. . . . Their skins were marked by the searing sun and dulled by the harsh weather which made deep furrows in their faces. Their hair was eaten away by bugs in the cereals. After years of this work, a man became a wreck, drained inside, nothing but an outer shell. Living in this hell, each year the docker takes another great stride towards his end. . . . Mechanization had superseded their physical capacity, only a quarter of them toiled away maintaining the pace of the machines, replacing the output of the unemployed workers.[17]

After working as a construction helper shamelessly exploited by his paternal uncle; after serving as a soldier in other people's war; after years of bearing the stigma of skin color in a segregated colonial world, now here was Sembène falling victim to a French capitalism that was slowly emerging, through the Marshall Plan, from the ruins of the war. Haunting images of the end of a day's work in the docks often convey the latent traumatic scenes imprinted in Sembène's memory: "When the sun had gone down and the day was well and truly over, the holds disgorged this human lava from their bowels. They walked with heavy step, hunched and broken with exhaustion. The damp smell of sweat rose from their bodies."[18] In such a work environment, frequent and serious accidents hardly came as a surprise. The alarming statistics reported by Robert Dubrou in the communist newspaper *La Marseillaise* only compound this sinister banality. According to Dubrou, there were 16,904 work accidents between 1950 and 1955. He also noted that bargemen[19] were little concerned about these figures.[20]

Sembène eventually paid the price of his employers' recklessness with regard to occupational safety and environment. Michel Libermann remembers the fateful event:

> It was in 1951, two years before the birth of my son Marc. Sembène had received a very heavy sack on his back. His backbone was fractured, and he spent weeks in the hospital, lying flat on his belly. After he checked out of the hospital, he had to wear a belt especially designed to straighten his backbone.[21]

The heavy sack fell on his back with such a violence that he was left with many vertebrae broken. Once again, death had cast its shadow over his life, but this time Sembène would not remain unscathed: for the rest of his life he would have to live with a horrible scar on his back and a slightly lopsided gait, with his body slanted to the right. But given all the difficult experiences he had been through, it is to be expected that Sembène would develop, over the years, a great capacity for resiliency in the face of physical pain. One incident, which occurred in Burkina Faso during the shooting of *Moolaade* in 2002, will be enough to substantiate this point about Sembène's resilience. After months spent trying to identify and locate sites for the movie, while transporting men and equipment in very rough conditions, Sembène had set up his headquarters in Sobara, in the southern province of Burkina Faso. For months, the 79-year-old man slept every single night on a tiny camping bed, when the temperatures were nearing 122°F, in a mosquito-infested area. None of this prevented him from working six days a week, between 9:00 AM and 6:00 PM. Not surprisingly, one day old Sembène simply fainted on the set, but in his typical fashion, he categorically refused to suspend the shooting, churlishly retorting to those who advised him to take a break and refill his batteries, "I'll have all the time needed to rest after my death." The harsh realities experienced on the Marseilles docksides had taught Sembène how to keep a project alive under precarious circumstances—unlike most pampered intellectuals who are easily upset and completely incapacitated by the slightest contingency. At La Joliette, he learned to value self-effacement and humility in an environment steeped in physical and psychological violence.

The brutality of slave societies described in Patrick Chamoiseau's *L'Esclave vieil homme et le molosse*[22] is strongly reminiscent of the bleak world in which the docker's life is embedded. For instance, there is what the Martiniquan writer calls *la décharge* (the release): to bring an end to his sufferings and humiliation, the Black slave reaches that extreme point where he wants to eliminate his own consciousness. This survival strategy consists in bracketing any inchoate desire for revolt, either physical or mental. At La Joliette, the proliferating bars and taverns were temples of self-destruction. As in the plantations of old, religion and alcohol were all-pervasive on the quaysides of the Marseilles harbor, fighting over the hearts and minds of these poor wretches who desperately wanted to forget everything, including their own selves. But no matter how one looks at it, the system only works with its victims' tacit consent. Most dockers thus ended up "shipwrecked" on a desert island made up of their thwarted ambitions and dashed hopes, constantly recalling images of their "idyllic" past. Sembène lived with those "castaways, swept along by the ocean of time."[23] Frequent brawls with the *patrons* (bar owners) or between workers provided an outlet for all the latter's heaped-up frustrations. In *Black Docker,* when Diaw Falla and N'Gor, the foreman, come to blows, Sembène painstakingly conveys this psychological dimension through their bodily movements:

> *Angered, Diaw sprang to his feet, gripped the fake marble table and with a sudden violent gesture sent it flying. It broke in two. . . . N'Gor stamped his feet. His wide nostrils were quivering. His breath came in a whistle. He was on guard, his fists clenched so tight they looked as if they might burst. His bloodshot eyes flashed.*[24]

Sembène did not fall into the trap of alcohol, thanks in large part to his acute political consciousness. "I don't know how to put it," confides Odette Arouh, another friend and comrade of Sembène's, "but since our first meeting I felt in Ousmane an inner strength that made him look special."[25] Sembène always seemed to cast a spell on those who approached him, fascinated by his strong personality, his determination, and his deep-seated belief that, as Simone Schwartz-Bart aptly put it, "life is a horse we must ride and not let it ride us."[26] However, there were periods of nagging self-doubt and overwhelming pressure, and this caused Sembène to experience the "release" Chamoiseau speaks of. It is that unpredictable moment when, to put things in a very trivial way, the lid suddenly bursts open with an irrepressible force. Although Sembène was too strong-minded to drift away, he could not refrain from giving vent to his anxieties and frustrations. Odette Arouh recounts: "Sometimes we would all go to a club, even though Sembène didn't really like to dance. On those occasions, he could, in a fit of anger, punch a bloody racist in the nose or any stupid jerk getting in his way."[27] Even in his old age, Sembène could still be quite brutal, at least verbally. Whenever he wanted to express a firm belief or simply a viewpoint, he was little concerned about *etiquette*—hence the reputation he earned himself as a terribly antisocial man, or even a slightly mad artist. One could argue, however, that this personality trait was due to his having seen many of his friends and co-workers wither away, physically or spiritually.

During his stay in Marseilles, Sembène managed to keep his soul unsullied by all the collateral effects of lumpenproletarization. According to his longtime friend Bernard Worms, "nothing distinguished him from the other African dockers, but he had something else: he was trying to improve his knowledge about the world. In this regard he was unique."[28] It must also be stressed that Sembène had to go through the whole educational line, since "he was practically illiterate," as Worms put it. However, Sembène did not reach the towering heights of his ambition by simply relying on his personal abilities. As Michel Libermann pointed out to me, "he was strongly supported, both emotionally and intellectually, by individuals and a group." In postwar Marseilles, Sembène found in the Vieux Port the key that would unlock the floodgate of his subversive creativity: labor militancy in the CGT, through which he drew closer to the communist left and to the socialist humanism later writ-large in the literary and cinematic works of a now full-fledged militant-artist.

13

The Militant

"*At the time,*" says Emile Belsenti, a retired docker, "the problem for us workers, was to be able, at least, to survive. You could no longer eke out a living with that job."[1] One would think that with the Marshall Plan, the situation would get better, but far from it: the plan made things worse. Like everybody else, Sembène struggled to keep his head above water, but these hard times also taught him the value of human solidarity: "When I arrived in Marseilles, I wanted to turn into a better person through hard work, and today I'm aware of the support many people gave me. I never miss an opportunity to pay a tribute to them."[2]

CGT, the powerful labor organization, provided the crucible on which was forged this ethic of proletarian brotherhood. If other organizations such as MRAP (Movement against racism and for friendship between peoples) also played a crucial role in the formative—and transformative—process of Sembène's intellectual growth, many individuals also left their "imprint" on his personal itinerary, including Victor Gagnaire, whom Sembène affectionately nicknamed "Papa Gagnaire." According to many of his contemporaries, Gagnaire, a charismatic union leader, was an ordinary worker who could hardly read; but he had the booming, spellbinding, and fiery voice of great orators. "Thanks to him, the harbor's union, which until 1935 had been controlled by the *patronat,* passed into the hands of the workers. The union thus evolved into a mass- and class-based democratic organization."[3] According to Marius Colombini, it was Gagnaire whom the communist Charles Tillon, then leader of the Fédération des Ports et Docks (Federation of harbors and docks) asked to reorganize the CGT-Unitaire (Unitary general confederation of labor). "Gagnaire was an extraordinary man," remembers Michel Libermann, "he was a former *Résistance* fighter, a generous man and a born leader." Gagnaire also led the dockers' strike in January 1936. Later on, and following a heart attack in 1962, he was elected honorary chairman of the union. He died as he had lived, one cold February morning, in 1963, on the docksides of La Joliette, while hawking the CGT newspaper, *La Vie Ouvrière* (Working life).[4]

CGT was created in 1895 as an umbrella organization bringing together a wide array of occupational groups. It was thus, in principle, an apolitical organization: "At CGT our main concern was the worker, and we really didn't give a damn whether a comrade was from the left, center or right. All that mattered was knowing to what extent he was ready to fight for the rights of workers," notes Belsenti. In actual fact, things were, obviously, not that simple. In its platform, CGT made no bones about its primary aim: "to defend the workers' economic interests." But since the organization came into being under the impetus of revolutionary trade unionism, its principles, as enshrined in the Amiens Charter, left no doubt as to its "political" goals and orientation. "The years 1948–1950 were turbulent and fraught with uncertainties," notes Pacini, "the Communist Party was so strong that it scared everybody stiff. In fact, beyond the claims for better working conditions, salaries and all that, we were really waging a political struggle. Clearly, for us it was all about establishing a new social order."[5] From its inception, CGT had been opposed to parliamentarianism and ultimately came to advocate a collectivization of the means of production. It was suspicious of any centralized state power and, like Gagnaire, most senior officials of the Union of Dockers, affiliated with CGT, were also prominent members of the French Communist Party. The latter had such a hold on union activities that in 1948, for example, some members decided to keep their distance from the union, so as to regain, as they put it, "their freedom of thought and initiative." The split resulted in the creation of CGT-Force Ouvrière (CGT-FO, General Federation of Labor—Labor Power), which was dominated by employees from the public administration and was headed, from 1948 to 1963, by Robert Bothereau.

At the time Ousmane Sembène joined CGT, it was, as already pointed out, the most powerful labor organization—and not only for dockers—in France, boasting six million card-holding members. Although Sembène was not the only African among the dockers, Gagnaire and the other senior officials quickly saw something special in this new recruit. To a certain extent, Sembène represented the ideal militant for the postwar French communist: an African from the colonies, a former colonial soldier and a lumpen proletarian; it was fairly easy to enlist him in the fight against capitalism and imperialism. But there was something else that elicited Gagnaire's interest: amidst the toiling multitude of the harbor's immigrant workers, Sembène was among the very few who wanted to increase their cultural capital. This bent of mind was an invaluable asset in that it made him more open than others to new ideas. Thus, Gagnaire's investment in the "Black docker" was both emotional and political. At the time, African workers were little aware of the root causes of their misery. They hardly perceived the forces at war in their host society, let alone the economic underpinnings of racism. In reality, they seemed to be little concerned about what was happening in France. Owing to their low levels of political and organizational awareness, they were sometimes instrumentalized as scabs by employers. Thus, getting these workers to rally round its banner became a matter of paramount importance for CGT.

Ousmane Sembène was well aware that the only salvation for his community resided in joining forces with French workers. This is evidenced by numerous passages in *Black Docker,* and Sembène himself confirmed to me this fact: "In addition to my work as a CGT union leader, I was also the secretary-general of Black workers in France. This enabled me to gain insight into both aspects, race- and class-based, of the situation. The way I saw it, it didn't make any sense that Africans living in Europe should try to set up a labor organization on the basis of their skin color. A labor organization is made up of workers from the same corporation fighting to improve their condition. When I arrived in Marseilles, CGT was a major entity and I joined it as a worker, without bothering to know whether there were in it Blacks like me or Yellows. Moreover, I saw in it a tool for self-improvement, for you learn an awful lot through trade unionism, it's a real school."[6] But while remaining open to this "universal" labor philosophy, Sembène also understood that genuine universality presupposed, first off, that all "workers of the world" be free. Consequently, countries under colonial rule had to gain their independence. Similarly, he was convinced that the Black worker's situation was tied to the liberation of Africa: "We were deep into the colonial era and we were strangers in France, to boot, on account of our culture and our language. It was therefore very difficult for us to create an organization. We had to situate our action within a political context, it was impossible to isolate ourselves," observes Sembène, before adding: "That said, when we returned to our neighborhood, we found back our roots through cultural activities that imbued us with a real sense of pride."[7] In the last analysis, Sembène fought on two fronts, and if he was so intent on acquiring more and more knowledge, it was also to make himself serviceable, as a revolutionary leader, to his African brothers living in France, whether they were Blacks or Arabs.

Moreover, in so doing Sembène was also inscribing himself within a firmly established Pan-African political tradition. It was not the first time a prominent Black figure was trying to rouse the continent from its slumber through an active involvement in European revolutionary trade unionism. Already in 1931, the Trinidadian George Padmore, a member of the German Communist Party and chairman of the International Trade Union Committee of Negro Workers, had initiated, from Berlin, a similar move. Proletarian organizations had come to the realization that it was crucial for them to attract Black workers living in Europe, most of whom were seamen and sailors. In a directive to the secretary of CGT-Unitaire, Padmore himself formulated unequivocally this absolute necessity: "We must consider it our central task to integrate Negro dockers and sailors from French harbors (Marseilles, Bordeaux, Le Havre) into revolutionary trade unions."[8] In the same letter, Padmore stressed the need "to choose Negro workers who will be groomed to become senior officials. . . . You shall endeavor to find sailors, for they are more connected to the colonies."[9] There was nothing unusual in Padmore's emphasis: he came from the West Indies and knew that these workers were less poisoned by colonial ideology than intellectuals. Likewise, Sembène held in deep contempt all those parliamentarians who wanted to become French at any cost. The writer admits he could never fathom such a deep-seated self-hatred: "It may have felt good to be a full-fledged French on paper, but when you were Black it was useless."[10] However, it would be unfair to sense in Sembène's dismissive attitude any narrow-mindedness. The internationalist ideal still provides the erstwhile docker with something like an ideological foothold, and when looking back on his past, he humbly acknowledged that "French workers fought alongside us and this helped us have some of our rights recognized."[11]

In spite of this solidarity, Sembène was well aware of the injustice African workers were experiencing, due to the iniquities inherent in the French legal system. He cites as an example family allowances in the 1950s: "If the wife of an African worker was in France, he would get 1,000 francs, like the French worker. But if his wife was in Africa, the amount went down to 400. The remaining 600 were deposited in whatever government fund, under the pretext that it was for the 'good' of the African worker. This was plain robbery, and it was unfair."[12] Talking about the history of the African labor movement and its relationship with CGT, Sembène explains,

> the situation in Africa, at the time, was quite different. The first organized action in Africa dates back to 1887, when a three-day strike was staged in Faidherbe's time. But it was only in 1910 that real struggles were waged. These revolts were violently quelled, and the cost in blood was always high. In 1938, there was the first movement of railroad workers, the ones you see in God's Bits of Wood. The strike was harshly repressed. After the war, there was a second movement, the victorious 1946 strike, which I partly recount in the same novel. This strike really gave birth to the labor movement. All the French-speaking countries took part in it, and we received help from CGT, the Soviet Union, Tchecoslovakia, etc. They all sent money to support us.[13]

Lamine Senghor, from Senegal, and Thiémoko Garang Kouyaté, from French Sudan (Mali), were, like Padmore, trailblazers on the road to an African labor movement. Lamine Senghor was born in 1889 into a peasant family and served as a colonial soldier during World War I. A low-ranking officer in the colonial army—he was a sergeant—, Senghor was gassed during a battle and eventually afflicted with tuberculosis, leading to his repatriation to Senegal in 1919. In 1921 he returned to France, where five years later he founded the Comité de Défense de la Race Nègre (Defense Committee of the Negro Race) and visited all the harbors between Fréjus and Marseilles to raise the political awareness of Black workers from Africa, the West Indies, and America. Senghor also formulated, with much foresight, the idea of a Pan-Africanism uniting all the downtrodden from Africa and its diaspora. Before his death in 1927, he was editing a newspaper, La Voix des Nègres, and had also made a claim to fame with the publication of a book on colonization in Africa, *La violation d'un pays* (The violation of a country). The struggle, both intellectual and political, of this African militant was carried on by Thiémoko Garang Kouyaté, a young Malian teaching in Ivory Coast who had come to study in Aix-en-Provence. Garang Kouyaté had joined the French Resistance during German occupation. In many respects, the life course of these two men prefigured Sembène's itinerary. Like Sembène, Senghor was a registered member of the Communist Party and had gained prominence as an activist in Black circles during the interwar period. But the two men have another thing in common: they never lost touch with their African roots, while being perfectly integrated into the French labor movement.

If for most, if not all, of its former proponents, communism has been consigned to the junkyard of ideologies since the fall of the Berlin Wall in 1989, Sembène continued to refuse to deny the ideal of his militant years. That ten-year period of activism (1951–1960) was engraved in a display case adorning his bedside in his old age, in which were neatly placed, in chronological order, the nine membership cards he held during that decade, looking like so many tutelary figures or charms. In the study room of his residence in Yoff, a life-size portrait of Lenin was mounted to the door. Some may frown upon all of this as old-fashioned communist pieties, or even joke about the "fetishism" of memorabilia, but Sembène's Marxism was never that of those *petit-bourgeois* intellectuals always desperate for some ideological thrill. He stepped into the social arena because he had no other choice. Only Sembène knew which excruciating hellhole these nine cards he beheld every morning took him out of; only he knew to what extent they gave him dignity and respect. However, it must also be stressed that Sembène, like Césaire before him, left the PC in 1960. He never again adhered to any political organization, devoting all his energies to literature and filmmaking. As he told Férid Boughedir in an interview: "I'm not a militant of any party, I'm a militant through my art."

Sembène's Marxist culture took shape within the context of CGT, a fact that Bernard Worms confirms: "When I met Ousmane in 1951, we were both CGT militants; he with the dockers in the harbor, and I in the academy, at the CNRS [National Center for Scientific Research]. At the time, being a labor militant wasn't the same as being a career soldier: the backbone wasn't enough, you had to be smart, you had to study real hard."[14] Sembène, for his part, underlines the educational environment set up by CGT: "At the time, reading was part of our union training. In the harbor, CGT had a library and all those who wanted to took free classes in its schools and in those of the PC."[15] Chaperoned by Gagnaire and the other senior officials, Sembène crammed to make up for lost time: political economy, social relations, modes of production, and so forth. In the last lines of *Black Docker*, as later in *God's Bits of Wood*, one can clearly sense Sembène's Marxist outlook:

> It is even more absurd to say that evil is not a product of the times. Where do murders, abortions, poisoning, theft, prostitution, alcoholism and homosexuality come from? From unemployment! There are too many unemployed! An accumulation of poverty: that is the root of all evil.[16]

As will be remembered, until his departure for the army in 1944 Sembène took events for granted, simply as they came, without acting upon them. Even his postwar "anti-colonial rage," as Maurice Fall calls it, was nothing but an impulsive, Pavlovian reaction, without any structuring political consciousness. Marxist theory, to which he was introduced during classes and debates in the union and the Party, was to give him this ideological and intellectual basis. More than once, Sembène made it clear that he totally adhered to this worldview. In 1971, speaking of *God's Bits of Wood*, unanimously hailed as his finest novel, he stated: "In *God's Bits of Wood*, I wanted to show that African unity cannot be envisioned outside of a Marxist purview." In 1996, Bernard Worms gave us some clues to an understanding of the importance of Marxism in the young docker's political thinking: "There is a symbiosis, in Sembène, between ways of thinking and ways of being, but not necessarily between ways of thinking and ways of dressing. For me, the real Sembène was the one who wrote *God's Bits of Wood*."[17]

Obviously, Sembène has never been particularly fond of his humiliating condition as a docker. But he always held the firm belief that man is a "work in progress" and that the road to self-improvement is primarily a matter of individual will. Bernard Worms bore witness to the inhuman and degrading conditions in which Africans in Marseilles, especially those in the harbor, lived and worked: "I'm of Jewish origin, a member of the MRAP, the PC, and of CGT. I was well acquainted with Sembène through these organizations. He was among those workers who were assigned the most repugnant tasks; but unlike all the others, Sembène was reading all the time. He was like a sponge, but he didn't merely imbibe knowledge. In fact Sembène was a 'processing' sponge." He was convinced that any real revolution must be foremost cultural. Sembène has a metaphor for this primacy of the cultural:

"Without culture, human beings are mere digestive tracts." In the militant circles of CGT and PCF, knowledge was seen as an instrument workers could not dispense with if they wanted to seize power. "We thought," continues Worms, "that another world was possible, and we were all confident that we only had to stay committed to achieve this. It all looked very simple: the triumph of the revolution was at hand, and to lead the world we had to gain as much knowledge as possible."[18]

Sembène's militant activities were embedded in a human environment that was congruent with his political and moral ideal. "Sure, Sembène possessed great individual qualities," observes Worms, "but these qualities couldn't have fully blossomed out if he hadn't been well integrated into a passionately intellectual environment."[19] Among the people who befriended Sembène during his Marseilles years, those who remember him best are his former comrades in the Party—who were often his best friends. In the '50s these two things went hand in hand: being active in the PC and living in a sort of second family. The Party provided emotional and welfare support; it also attended to everyone's existential problems. "Ideology didn't merely serve as a common denominator," emphasizes Michel Libermann, "it also served as a 'code of civility' in our political interactions. We were thus not obsessed with the notion of difference. We were all the more disinclined toward xenophobia that MOI, the Main d'Oeuvre Immigrée (Immigrant labor power), which was made up of foreign communists, had been at the forefront of the *Résistance*."[20] The rejection of racism was so deeply entrenched in this universe that some harbor workers in Marseilles had been shocked by the title of Sembène's first novel, for "there could be neither a Black docker, nor one who was white, red or whatever else color. There was just a *docker*, and that was that."[21] At least, joked some, there could be "yellow" dockers, a sarcastic allusion to the scabs who had sold out to the bourgeoisie.

In a larger context, this notion of a human community transcending race and nationality is one of the core beliefs shared by all communists. "It mattered little to me that Sembène was Black or African; what struck me most in him was that he was a *honnête homme,* in the Enlightenment sense of someone who had learned much from various cultural experiences," underlines Michel Libermann, before adding, with a wry smile, "but to tell you the truth, for me Sembène is first of all a native of Provence, of Marseilles!" To illustrate his point about the cosmopolitanism prevailing during that period, Bernard Worms likes to cite his own case as an example: "I was rejected by my father, who was a Jew, and my mother, a Catholic! Ultimately,

I'm neither the one nor the other, but all the same, I claim them both. Don't ask me why! Sembène and I were active in organizations fighting against anti-Semitism, because in our communist environment there was this need and desire to reach out to the Other. Our motto was 'solidarity and fraternity in the struggle.' *Cégétistes*[22] or not, we were rich with our utopia and a practical humanism today people tend to see, with hindsight, as rather naïve. Still, there were genuine human interactions between us, the kind communism dreamed to see the whole world embrace, although now one can say that the flower buds have not blossomed into full-fledged flowers."[23] This failure to make the dream come true, alluded to in such a veiled manner by the old communist, had been hard to come to terms with for many other comrades. Seeing all their dreams smashed against the "iron wall" of reality, many sank deep into despair and depression. Sembène never entertained, even once, the thought of forswearing his communist allegiance, and his combativeness remained intact.[24] Since that period he held racism, sexism, and xenophobia beneath contempt. Sembène's encounter with the postwar communist left was for him a genuine human experience; he drew from it an unwavering faith in the future happiness and prosperity of humankind. But more crucially for Sembène and his generation, there was this firm belief that the well-being of everyone had to be the work of all. This is not to say that the fate of a community must be entrusted to some providential hero, nor is it an invitation to waste oneself away in sterile dreams; as Sembène himself put it in his oft-repeated witty remark: "Me I don't dream, I'm too down to earth, you know." Freedom, once wrenched away from the powers that be, can only be preserved through struggle. The most recent works of the writer-director celebrate, in images beautifully conveying these human truths, this culture of resistance inextricably tied to a deep sense of honor. The man one often heard say in Wolof: *bañ gàcce, nangu dee* (I'll say no to humiliation, I'll say yes to death) could have easily adopted Mao Tse-tung's old revolutionary dictum: "It is always right to revolt."

Yet when Sembène left Dakar, there was no hint of the radical metamorphosis to come—although he showed some signs of it during his brief spell in the army. If he has become such a potent "processor of worlds," it is because in Marseilles he had been through crucial experiences that enabled him to find his Truth. Childhood experiences are often used as a kind of Rosetta stone through which one attempts to decipher the hieroglyphs of one's adult life, but as we all know, the palimpsest of the past is fraught with bogus and deceptive traces. Perhaps one should agree with Antoine de Saint-Exupéry that men rise to superhuman levels only in extreme, borderline situations: "We have known shopkeepers who, in the course of a long night spent bearing with the hardships of a shipwreck or fighting a fire, have revealed themselves to be greater than they thought.... This will remain the most momentous night of their life. But for lack of new occasions, propitious conditions, for lack of a demanding religion, they have gone back to sleep, without believing in their own greatness."[25]

That watershed moment may well have been, in Sembène's case, the famous unlimited strike unanimously voted on March 10, 1950, by the Union of Dockers. But they had it rough then. Irving Brown, a CIA agent sent to France to wage a clandestine war against communism, had funded the creation of Force Ouvrière (Labor Power). CGT militants had long since labeled this splinter group, which had the support of Pierre Ferri-Pisani, the deputy mayor of Marseilles, a "yellow"[26] union. During the strike, the dockers had thus to contend with extremely powerful lobbies. Bernard Worms, who experienced the events firsthand, remembers: "At the time a secretary-general of a trade union wasn't the kind of cold technocrat he has become today. He was a fiery orator who could also get rough and punch in the nose a dissenter or a scab."[27] With such hot-blooded leaders, ready for a fight, a strict discipline was *de rigueur*. "We obeyed these men like robots, but you couldn't call it sheepishness. We respected them because they had often put their lives on the line, the eldest during the Great War and the others during the *Résistance*," adds Worms. In light of these statements, one can better understand some of Sembène's attitudes, notably on his movie sets. He continued to believe so firmly in the virtues of rigid authority that his collaborators often criticized him of being "too authoritarian," but the filmmaker was little bothered by the complaint, having spent his whole career shouting to such and such an actor or technician: "I dispense you from thinking; I'm just asking you to do what I tell you to do, that's all." This was always said in a half-serious, half-sarcastic tone, and Sembène's old age mitigated whatever may be shocking in this attitude, especially with African interlocutors. The director jokingly called it his peculiar brand of "enlightened despotism," but one must not forget that he received a typical Stalinist training. Bernard Worms tacitly acknowledges this: "In the PC, it was the same as with the Jesuit fathers, one had to obey like a corpse in the hands of the washer." Of course, things have changed now, one cannot be as dogmatic, but such a state of mind is bound to stick with you like a leech.

However, one must interpret these Sembenian "antics" in light of the political events of that period. CGT took an active part in overseas anticolonial movements. A novel such as *God's Bits of Wood* shows that labor struggles were not limited to defending the narrow and immediate interests of the dockers. Sembène was particularly fond of this "something more" that is beyond the pale of any militant praxis and lay buried deep inside of him—albeit more in his heart than in his mind. He absolutely needed to feel like a world citizen battling injustice all over the globe.

Such was the case in Algeria, where the bloody repression of the 1945 Sétif uprising led to the creation, two years later, of the National Liberation Front (FLN). The first uprisings staged within the context of the Algerian War of Liberation took place in Kabylia, in 1954. As would be expected, the "events in Algeria," as they were euphemistically called by colonialists in the metropole, had a deep impact on French society. CGT dockers in Marseilles supported FLN in the name of a principled solidarity with all the oppressed. In any case, they had a number of reasons to feel concerned about this war: geographical proximity, political stakes, and Algeria's economic influence. At the time, Marseilles was already home to the bulk of the Algerian community in France. For Sembène, supporting these people was not mere sloganeering but a concrete gesture of humanity, for he rubbed shoulders with countless "Chaïbas" along the putrid gutters of his street, the Rue des Dominicaines. The presence of Algerians in large numbers had greatly contributed to turning this "Tanga Sud," located in the "deep south" of France, into the hub of colonial economy. From the mid-1940s until his return in Senegal in 1960, Sembène intimately knew that this exemplary war of liberation was also about him. Its emancipatory echoes reverberate throughout the early works and in *Camp de Thiaroye,* the long feature film which he co-directed with Thierno Faty Sow in 1988. It was no coincidence that Algeria participated in the movie's production: the Thiaroye massacre is strongly reminiscent, image after image, of the Sétif repression. For all these reasons, Sembène's ties with progressive Algerian artists remained strong and healthy.[28]

Sembène also took part, in his own militant way, in the Indochina War. When, in August 1945, Ho Chi Minh proclaimed the independence of the Democratic Republic of Vietnam, he was still a French soldier in the Sixth Colonial Infantry Regiment. From Niger, some of his comrades were sent to Indochina. After fighting against German troops, they were being coerced into serving as agents of French colonial repression. One had to be deaf and blind not to see through the French state's tactics—and this was far from being Sembène's case. Here too, he knew how to make himself serviceable to a people in struggle. Owing to its position on the Mediterranean coastline, the harbor in Marseilles was strategically crucial for the movement of troops and military equipment from the metropole to Indochina. Workers in the harbor could thus strongly exert an influence over what was happening on the battlefields. CGT had no choice but to support the Viet Minh, which claimed a Marxist orientation. Moreover, the dockers bore witness, every day, to the horrors of that war, as wounded soldiers from Indochina were repatriated through Marseilles. During the four months—from March 13 to July 21, 1954—that the French last-ditch offensive on Dien Bien Phu lasted, Ousmane Sembène and his comrades sided with the Viet Minh. Sembène's fiction recreates this experience through numerous characters. It is worth noting that in the novelist-director's works, the war veteran, a living proof of the trauma resulting from a colonial conflict, is always a "mentally disturbed" person.[29]

Sembène's personal involvement in the war also took the form of a brief appearance as an extra in *Le Rendez-vous des quais* (1953, Rendez-vous on the docksides), by the Marseilles-born communist director Paul Scarpita, a movie celebrating the solidarity between CGT dockers and Indochinese revolutionaries. Censors were so infuriated that the movie's only copy was seized in 1955, on the very night of its world premiere. *Le Rendez-vous des quais* tells the story of a young couple in postwar Marseilles. The man is a docker and the woman works in a candy factory. Life is hard and they cannot find an apartment. On the quays, after the dead and wounded from Indochina have been hauled off the ship, the latter is freighted with cannons and tanks. Strikes burst out, the police intervene. To survive and find an apartment, the movie's hero, Robert Fournier, betrays his struggling comrades to join the "yellow" trade union. It must be pointed out that the movie would have never been completed without the generous participation of CGT dockers. One can also assess the impact of the war in Indochina on Sembène's artistic work, through his readiness to keep alive the memory of African soldiers' sacrifice. Thus, in the dedication to *Vehi Ciosane, or Blanche Genèse*, published in 1966 (as *White Genesis, with the Money Order*, 1972), Sembène honors the memory of Sarr Pathé: "[Sarr Pathé] was one of the companions of my youth. Together we underwent the ordeal of initiation. He believed in the God of *Gain*, in happiness through *Money*. After the '39–'45 war, he enlisted in the French Expeditionary Corps. He died penniless in Indochina, in June '54. My old friend Boca Mbar,[30] Sarr Pathé."[31]

The 1950–1953 Korean War also elicited Sembène's ever-keen interest. It was—and is still, with North Korea listed among the "rogue states"—an ideological showdown of global proportions. A local colonial war of liberation, such as in Algeria and Indochina, pales in comparison. What was at stake in Korea was nothing less than the reinforcement—or weakening—of the communist bloc in the Cold War context. The issue was hotly debated in Marseilles circles. Sembène's rare interventions during these meetings commanded general attention and respect. According to Worms, he always voiced his overriding concern: the unity in action between immigrant workers and metropole progressives. It was this Sembène, who harbored a deep-seated hostility toward all kind of sectarianism, who was active as an antiracist militant in MRAP.

Carrying on the tradition of the French Revolution and the progressive militancy of men like Abbé Grégoire, MRAP was created to fight against the century-old Christian anti-Semitism still plaguing Europe, the racially devastating consequences of the Slave Trade and, broadly speaking, against European colonialism. In late nineteenth-century France, during colonial expansion, this campaign for tolerance, conducted in a spirit of active resistance, was crystallized around the Dreyfus affair.[32] Created in 1941 and resulting indirectly from resistance to Nazism, the National Movement against Racism (MNCR) became the Jewish Coalition against Racism, Anti-Semitism and for Peace (UJRAP). This anti-Vichy organization saved many Jewish children from deportation. From 1949 on, to be in line with Cold War realities, MRAP evolved out of UJRAP and drew closer to the communists. When Sembène joined the movement, its headquarters were on the last floor of a building located on 43, Rue du Tapis Vert. On the same floor were also located the offices of the Jewish Youth of Marseilles, which consisted of a bunch of progressive organizations. Ousmane Sembène and William Fall, a Senegalese sailor, were the only Africans active as MRAP militants. As with the harbor's trade union and the PC, Sembène gained acquaintance with men and women who would play a major role in his political and artistic training, notably Odette Arouh. In 1954, the year they met, she was 20 and Sembène had turned 31. *Black Docker* was dedicated to this young Jewish woman—who would become the godmother of his son Alain, born in Marseilles—and Ginette Constantin. For Ousmane Sembène, Odette was more than a comrade and a friend, she was almost like a sister: "Sembène often came to our house on Rue Sainte-Catherine, where Ginette also lived. We were a group of friends from the Jewish neighborhood of Marseilles, always dead broke. Sembène also endeared himself to my father, whom he called Papa Rouh. We were real militants, but we also liked to hang out in clubs. We held meetings in youth hostels. In our circle, which was on the far left side of the political spectrum, we held racism in such deep contempt, you could even say we had blinkers, for all those who weren't like us held no interest for us. We wanted to be in solidarity with all the oppressed people on earth. The day the Black McGee[33] was hanged in the United States, I remember spending the whole evening writing a poem on him. We were that romantic."[34]

Bernard Worms attempts to explain Sembène's trajectory in light of this state of mind, typical of the left in the 1950s:

> I've been active as a militant since 1946–1947, and I've known Sembène in the Communist Party, then CGT and MRAP. For us the phenomenon "Sembène" was, so to speak, part of the natural order of things. The period was, for good or ill, Stalinist; we made it a point to have our way of life conform in all respects to our ideas; if you claimed to be an internationalist, you couldn't be a racist, that wouldn't make sense. So Sembène was just one of us, no one paid attention to the color of his skin. Of course, it's only when we see what's going on today that we realize how naïve we must have been. But you have to remember that in France, it was only after World War II that Marxism started to dominate the political landscape. When people emerge from such a deadly conflict, their consciousness is on the alert, they dream about a better world and are therefore willing to embrace all kinds of utopia. Sembène is a product of this Marxist humanism and of this staunchly anti-colonialist period.[35]

It was also within the context of MRAP's struggles that Sembène strengthened his friendship with the former resistance fighter Michel Libermann and his wife, Janine: "I met Sembène," says Libermann, "through Odette, at MRAP, of which I was a co-founder. I'm also of Jewish origin, although now I'm an atheist. My wife's parents died in deportation. Sembène introduced us to the African milieu in Marseilles. With him we sold MRAP's newspaper, *Droits et Libertés* [Rights and liberties], on Rue du Tapis Vert, in Belsunce. He often came to dinner at our house on Avenue Camille Peltin, along with the rest of the group."[36]

At MRAP, Sembène took part, among other matters, in support actions for the Rosenbergs. Defense committees were set up all over the world and Michel Libermann chaired the one in Marseilles. From 1951 to 1953, he and Sembène organized demonstrations in solidarity with Julius and Ethel

Rosenberg, two New York Jews falsely accused of spying for Soviet Russia. Although there was clearly an anti-Semitic dimension to it, the trial must be situated within the Cold War context. The son of a Polish Jew, Julius Rosenberg was a member of the City College of New York's Young Communist League. After graduating as an electrical engineer, he was recruited by the U.S. Army in 1940, at a time when the United States was developing a nuclear bomb program, the infamous "Manhattan Project," at the Fort Alamos National Laboratory. Julius Rosenberg and his wife, Ethel, who was charged with complicity, were convicted and executed on June 19, 1953. The execution came as a terrible shock to Sembène, and today one can understand the extent to which he must have been saddened by the emotion that would overwhelm him at the mere mention of the couple's names. I can bear witness to this, for the day I asked him about the trial, I saw Sembène, for the one and only time ever, on the verge of tears. Instead of answering my question, he remained silent for a few seconds before diverting the flow of conversation to another topic.

In this militant environment, Sembène was also deeply influenced, politically and artistically, by Henri Cohen, secretary-general of the Union des Juifs pour la Résistance et l'Entraide (Jewish coalition for resistance and mutual help). A hunchback and an almost dwarfish figure, Cohen was a highly educated man and a great *Résistance* fighter who had completed his high school studies in Marseilles. With Gabriel Péri, former chief editor of the communist newspaper *L'Humanité,* Cohen had founded his own organization, Les étudiants communistes (Communist students). Opposed to fascism during the war, Péri was executed by the Nazis. Libermann sketched a portrait of Henri Cohen for us: "A great militant, Henri was a guy who, because of his vast culture, had a tremendous influence on us. Sembène had known him and like me, he learned a lot from him through long and passionate discussions on literature, painting and cinema."[37] But Sembène also learned much in youth hostels, notably the one in Fantaque Saint-Cassis, a small fishing harbor near Marseilles, on the Souberane cliffs. "That hostel," remembers Bernard Worms, "was where we had all-night sessions with young people from all over the world; an ever lively place, it also hosted our postwar political clashes. It was a place to learn together how to cope with life."[38]

As is amply shown by all these trade union and political activities, Ousmane Sembène had all the credentials of the typical postwar Bolshevik militant. However, he was soon to have strong misgivings about the leadership role of the Communist Party. He also sensed in Soviet Russia's attitude toward colonized peoples residual traces of paternalism, inasmuch as its own vested interests dictated any support it provided. In any event, with the wars in Algeria and Indochina, Sembène had come to the realization that self-reliance is the key to liberation. He showed more openness toward an application, *mutatis mutandis*, of Marxist principles to the African situation. In short, he was willing to appropriate the famous formula: "A little patriotism weakens internationalism, much patriotism strengthens it." Paradoxically, it was through the lens of Marxist humanism that he better perceived the specificity of Africa, then still under colonial rule and on the margins of the world.

Thus in 1956, Sembène composed his first poem, "Liberté" (Freedom), in which a man's dream and the project of his life are given full expression. After paying tribute to China, India, the Viet-Minh, Soviet Russia, the United States and, most particularly, France, Sembène lucidly comes to grips with his own ambiguous situation:

And yet in all these lands not once
Shall I feel at home.
In all these arrays of beings, of culture,
And language:
I'm ignored . . . cast into oblivion.
Alone the name of my country
Rings a bell
O . . . my country!
My country, my Island,
My beautiful Island . . .

We have been subdued
By the weak arm and sterile mind of the conqueror
He deals only in blows
He spreads only calumnies.

Our sons of old—sold as slaves—
Will return.
Today, out of the living people
We shall shape, in the mold of solidarity, dedication:
A nation.[39]

In the "Village," everyone knew the "Black docker" from Senegal, especially in the community and mutual help organizations Sembène helped set up.

For example, there was the Association des ressortissants d'AOF/AEF (Association of nationals from French West Africa and French Equatorial Africa), whose goal was to support immigrants from African colonies. From 1956 to 1959, Sembène had been secretary-general of that organization, where workers and intellectuals—notably students—interacted and shared their experiences. The organization was mainly a means of involving all Africans living in France in independence movements. We do not know at what exact date Sembène started to move in the circles of African intellectuals in Marseilles. We can just venture to say that *Black Docker,* published in 1956, had been his entry ticket to those circles. His double status as a worker and a writer put him in an ideal position to reconcile two mutually exclusive universes.

Although World War II divided the world into two camps, it also accelerated the emergence of a wide network of nationalist movements going confrontational with the then beleaguered colonial powers. In Africa, the 1945–1960 interval was one of ideological confrontation and political turmoil. While as early as 1944 de Gaulle had trumpeted his firm resolution to keep the French empire intact, on the African continent, and even in France, workers, peasants, and politicians had come to the realization that this war had ushered in a new era. At this point in our account of Sembène's life, it is perhaps worthwhile to review key issues and, so to speak, take a look at the "mileage gauge": it has gradually emerged that Sembène's itinerary and rich militant experience made him stand out as a leader of the African immigrant community in Marseilles. Now this can help us understand how in 1957, he was to be among the co-founders of the Marseilles chapter of PAI (African Independence Party). As we have seen, before he left for France in 1946, and even during his childhood in Ziguinchor, Sembène had always been in contact with African politicians. It was, to a certain extent, a family affair, as Galandou Diouf's followers would convene at the house of Moussa Sembène. His son never mentions this fact without adding a typically Sembenian, slightly rude comment, to the point of calling the old man a "rogue."[40] Sembène's participation in the liberation of France left him with many unanswered questions: "First we were told that we were defending our fatherland with Pétain. . . . The next day, Pétain was overthrown and I found myself fighting as a Gaullist." When Sembène was demobilized, he bitterly realized two things at once: colonial authorities wanted to return to the *status quo ante,* whereas for Africans the hour of liberation had finally come. "After the war, a new spirit was blowing through the air, in Dakar,"[41] affirmed Sembène, referring to the postwar trade union and political effervescence.

Thousands of people would attend Lamine Guèye's first meetings, but Sembène despised this SFIO representative, who was a hardcore assimilationist. This hardly comes a surprise, for indeed Guèye's political organization was merely the "African chapter" of a metropolitan party, SFIO. A representative at Palais-Bourbon (France's "Capitol Hill"), Lamine Guèye was not the only one to champion assimilation since, according to Sembène, "it was a claim staked by the whole Senegalese intelligentsia, it even predated World War I. . . . To repeat: at the time independence wasn't the issue, it was all about fighting for French citizenship."[42]

Sembène had also witnessed the birth of the African Democratic Alliance (RDA) in 1946. The event had aroused much hope in the colonies, for it was the first time that a political party was created in Africa, for Africans and by Africans. This was, for Sembène, the kind of "sacred alliance" between Africans that the continent desperately needed to shake off its colonial shackles. He had followed with keen interest the discussions that led to the Bamako meeting: "This was happening in Dakar, in my neighborhood. I had only to push open our entrance door to find myself in the midst of a big political rally!"[43] However, the speeches that were then delivered went "over the top of his head," and Sembène readily conceded it: "As if on cue, all these people had to come and talk politics right under my window. I thus found myself in a situation that overwhelmed me, to be honest with you. I wanted to take the floor, too, but I was illiterate and had to rest content with listening to these parliamentarians everybody admired."[44] This frustration was already mixed with a strong reservation, of ominous significance: "In my inmost being I disagreed with what I heard, but I had no counter-argument to put forward. . . ."[45] As it was avowedly fighting for the self-determination and unity of the continent, no sooner was RDA created than it had the unconditional backing of the French Communist Party. But the alliance was short-lived, as Félix Houphouët-Boigny severed all ties with the PC after his liberal turn—when he started preaching the gospel of liberalism in Ivory Coast and all over the African continent.

Sembène's duties in community organizations led him to take an interest in the actions of men like Léopold Sédar Senghor and Félix Houphouët-Boigny. Sembène neither liked, nor trusted them at all, as can be seen in the introductory note to God's Bits of Woods. According to him, African deputies in Paris were mere byproducts of the colonial system, and as such they were ill-equipped to effect radical changes in the life of Africans. To him, it was rather naïve to expect this intellectual elite to relinquish its privileges and saw off the cozy little branch on which its members were—and are still—sitting. Sembène claims to have reached this conclusion during strikes against the war in Indochina. "It was Vietnam War, you know, and it made me come to grips with the crude fact of colonialism. It was then I realized, unlike most of our intellectuals, that what was at stake in our struggle was primarily economic, not cultural. . . . I wanted to say things, but I didn't have yet the opportunity to formulate them."[46] In his own way, Sembène would later exact a sweet revenge in "Communauté" (The Union), a short story included in the collection *Voltaïque*.[47] The story is written in the allegorical vein that is Birago Diop's stylistic signature. It is about a "union scheme" between cats and rats in a "political entity" clearly suggestive of de Gaulle's Communauté Française (French union). "Upon his return from Mecca, the rat El Hadji Niara set out to launch a vast preaching campaign to convert all his fellow rats and create a larger community."[48] How did it all end up? As can be easily inferred, to the great detriment of the rats. "'Woe unto the infidels!,' he [El Hadji Niara] shouted to his followers. There ensued a general melee . . . The few surviving rats . . . sneaked into their holes again. The next morning, many rats were missing." And the narrator concludes: "Since that day, rats refuse to embrace any belief or join any community; and from that day on, they have been devising these little safety holes."[49]

Sembène ultimately adopted a very hostile attitude toward those who propounded a step-by-step independence process, RDA's famous gradualism. He was in favor of a radical break, pure and simple. Independence was to herald a new Africa, made up of free nations:

As it arose between daybreak and the clear morning light,
The wind swept down on the buds,
A nefarious, shadow-casting blow;
The night of dark ignorance is fading out,
And the rejuvenated souls and minds
Will soon be reunited
Like sticks in a bundle of wood.

This nascent dawn
Will bend the steel force of weapons,
At the high noon of our freedom.[50]

In Sembène's eyes, the ideal of freedom could be found in forces that were far bolder and more assertive than Houphouët-Boigny's RDA or

Lamine Guèye's SFIO chapter. This was one of the reasons behind his active involvement in the Federation of French West African Students (FEANF), created in 1950 at the start of the Korean War. FEANF, which brought together students from AOF, AEF, Togo, and Cameroon, played a key role in the fight for the independence and unity of African countries under French domination—and this was all the more significant that most African leaders, at the time, had refused to fight for total independence. In 1953, Présence Africaine, the review founded in 1947 by Alioune Diop, published a special issue entitled "Les étudiants africains parlent" (Black students speak out). It was the first time the injunction to fight for total independence was publicly voiced on behalf of FEANF: "L'unique issue: l'indépendance totale. La seule voie: un large mouvement anti-impérialiste,"[51] such was the title of the text associated with this radical branch. Its author, Majmout Diop, was a medical student who would eventually found PAI, a Marxist-inspired political party, in 1957. In Marseilles, Sembène set up chapters for PAI and PAIGC (African party for the independence of Guinea-Bissau and Cape Verde, also created in 1957). In August 1959, following the massacre of 50 striking Bissau Guineans in the Pidjiguti harbor,[52] Sembène immediately created a section of the Mouvement de Libération de la Guinée et du Cap-Vert (Movement for the liberation of Guinea-Bissau and Cape Verde) and organized fundraising activities for the victims' families. Thus, Sembène played a quite significant role in the political awakening of Africans in France, especially on the eve of independences. He also greatly contributed to improving the relations between African immigrants and PCF. The latter included, among its registered members, labor leaders or students from French Guinea and Mali, but also members of the Overseas and Afro-Malagasy Regional Federation (FRAMOM).

However, this exceptional political trajectory is constantly overshadowed by the writer-director's artistic corpus. Perhaps we are inclined to think that only his artistic work will be preserved in the cultural memory of humankind. And yet Sembène himself never separated these two parts of himself: "I'm both an artist and a militant," he would say emphatically, "but I'm not a member of any political party. I'm a militant through my art." It took Sembène a long time before he could discard his orthodox Marxist views and acknowledge the primacy of the cultural over the economic. This revisionary assessment, however painful, enabled Sembène to re-inscribe his eminently political sphere of agency, beyond the pale of the here and now, in the continuity of history.

14

The Fire-Giver

Ousmane Sembène, the erstwhile docker, will no doubt leave a rich legacy to posterity. Through his work, he has been one of the most prominent Africans of his time. To provide just one example, his last movie, *Moolaade,* made when he was already past his eighties, conquered the most diverse audiences; it also represents Sembène's strongest statement as to his exceptional vitality as a man and an artist. This long career has been marked by scores of prestigious awards from all over the world (see "Biographical Landmarks"). With regard to the numerous distinctions he has earned, one must recognize the fact that Sembène owed a great deal of his international notoriety to cinema. But does this necessarily entail that he thought of himself more as a filmmaker than a writer, that he wholeheartedly cast the latter identity into the background? It would be misleading to view things in terms of the primacy of one over the other, for Sembène's artistic practice is entirely dictated by pragmatic considerations: "In the current situation of chronic illiteracy prevailing in Africa, it's more pragmatic to make a movie than to write a novel. With cinema, I can reach more people in one night than any preacher in a mosque or a church, or any politician during a meeting. But cinema can turn us all into dumb-heads: it blots out the horizon, dulls the imagination and holds us *captive*[1] within the narrow confines of a movie theater. With literature you have more freedom, you can caress the pages, stop or go back over a previous passage; literature makes you feel things. Personally, I prefer literature to cinema."[2] To put it differently: for years the necessities of cultural politics in Africa forced Sembène to repress a burning desire for writing that can be traced back to his childhood. As will be remembered, in the 1930s Abdourahmane Diop, the uncle in Marsassoum, Casamance, exerted a sort of magnetic pull over his nephew.

Sembène claimed to be the only one in his family who escaped illiteracy, but this is only a partial truth, for many of his relatives, on the maternal side, were schooled either in French or in Arabic. This was quite unusual, especially in Casamance, where education was a privilege reserved for an elite consisting of colonial employees from other regions of Senegal, mostly from the Four Communes. Sembène was certainly a self-taught man, but he did not land in Marseilles like a traveler unequipped for his journey. In addition to his family heritage, the young Sembène also drew on his passion for reading and cinema to get some informal training. His brief passage in *Ecole de la Rue de Thiong* would also prove a rewarding experience, and the Plateau in Dakar, where Africa's political future was being shaped, also gave him countless intellectual opportunities, including the *kasag, fanal,* and cultural night sessions held in the old Lebu settlements of Mboth and Thiédem.

However, nothing Sembène experienced during his Dakar years can stand the comparison with his eye-opening encounter with the seventh art: "In the beginning, when we went to the outdoor movie theater, I sometimes hid behind the screen to see where the characters appearing in the movie were coming from." In the short story "Devant l'histoire" (Facing history), published in 1962, Sembène powerfully recreated the atmosphere of that period:

> *They [the three friends] were in front of Le Mali. All three intently fixed their gaze on the long line that increased by the minute, as men, women and children came in droves. On the edge of the luminous halo, street vendors and women selling snacks had arranged their small tables. Prostitutes strolled around. The air was cool, less torrid than the city. Every now and then a wind blew from the neighborhood, bringing with it the putrid smell of decayed matter.*[3]

Indulging in escapism was quite to be expected from someone his age, but Sembène's behavior also portended his future awakening. He was learning about the world so as to better know how to change it, and this philosophical "project" soon led him to orient his readings toward a more and more specific direction. This is evidenced by his strong misgivings about the politicians of that period and their rabble-rousing speeches. As previously noted, the speeches delivered "right under [his] window" left Sembène deeply perplexed, but it was precisely at that point he had something close to an epiphanic moment: "I wanted to talk back to [the politicians] but I was illiterate. I knew I couldn't counter them, because I had no argument to put forward. This is why I decided to leave for France. I wanted to get a good education and learn more about the world."[4] Which city in the world other than Marseilles, the "Red City," could have suited him better?

Marseilles did not wait until the German occupation of France to tap into its cultural resources. The '30s were marked by an extraordinary outburst of creativity in all domains. The old neighborhood of L'Arsenal des Galères was home to many poets and painters. Under Jean Ballard's leadership, the literary review *Cahiers du Sud* was back in circulation. At the Ecole Jean Renoir, Marcel Pagnol was starting a movie production company. At the theater Le Rideau Gris, Louis Ducreux and André Roussin were also doing a fantastic job. In 1925, Gaston Berger founded the Société d'Etudes Philosophiques (Philosophical Society of Marseilles); and in 1929 the Institut Historique de Provence (Provence Historical Institute) had come into being, headed by professors Eugène Duprat and Jean Masson. All of this bore witness to the emergence of a new generation of intellectuals, and public opinion's rapid shift to the left was quite symptomatic of this. Thus, starting in 1935, an electoral agreement between the Communist Party and the department's socialist federation catapulted SFIO's Henri Tassot into the mayoral seat. But the 1940 debacle halted this political dynamic. The whole country was devastated, and although France would eventually regain its leadership as a world power, this blitz defeat of the army dealt a hard blow to its morale. Historian and urban sociologist Jean-Michel Guiraud, who lived through this period, sees in the debacle the onset of a two-year-long cultural lethargy: "Everything seemed suspended; passive resistance activities hurled the city into darkness; the city's monuments disappeared behind rafters and bulwarks of sandbags; museums, libraries and the Opéra were closed. The whole Provence was putting to safety its works of art, shoved into hermetic boxes, loaded onto trucks."[5] Fortunately, Marseilles was the only non-occupied harbor, and the city quickly regained its status as a cultural hub. All converged on Marseilles: anti-fascist intellectuals and artists from all over the world; persecuted Jews and communists. Paul Valéry, Simone Weil, André Breton, Anna Seghers, and Claude Lévi-Strauss graced the offices of *Cahiers du Sud* with their occasional visits. This vibrant cultural life was partly due to the existence, in Marseilles, of an American Committee set up to evacuate all those who incurred the risk of being handed over to the Nazis, as stipulated by an agreement between Germany and the Vichy regime. German novelist Thomas Mann was one of the first to be evacuated to the United States, from Marseilles. However, the Committee failed to do the same for André Malraux, Chagall, or Picasso. On January 16, 1943, the *Luftwaffe* bombed the city, and the whole Zone Sud was subsequently occupied. A new chapter in Marseilles's history began. Until its liberation in May 1944, the city would be the site of a fierce resistance put up by CGT, then a clandestine organization; socialist militias; PCF-affiliated MOI (Immigrant Labor Power); and the Organization of Armed Resistance—better known as la Résistance.

After the war, history took another dramatic turn, as Marseilles found itself at a crossroads between France in search of its new—or irretrievably lost—identity, and the incipient bipolar world of the Cold War. Russia controlled Eastern Europe and Harry Truman launched the Marshall Plan, designed to close the ranks in his own camp, the West. In France, General de Gaulle founded the Rassemblement du Peuple Français (French People's Alliance) in 1947 and five communist ministers were expelled from the Ramadier cabinet. This decision came as a shock to many, for until then PCF had been rather accommodating. For instance, since 1945 it had adopted a reformist stance so as to help improve productivity. Following its eviction, PCF stirred things up again on the social front, capitalizing on the growing discontent resulting from frequent shortages and price inflation. In that year, 1947, rampant and endemic strikes crippled the entire French economy. Sembène had been part of this period of struggle, but it was not his first direct contact with communism. He tells the story of how he seized numerous opportunities to listen to Marxist intellectuals in postwar Dakar: "Professors like Suret-Canale came to talk to us about Marx and Lenin. I think this was my first school. Then there was the railroad workers' strike."[6] French intellectuals and artists immediately reacted to the Cold War, either by openly siding with de Gaulle's RPF, like Malraux, or by seeking a middle ground, like Sartre, who famously styled himself a "fellow-traveler" of communism. As for Sembène, he made no bones about his allegiance to the communist camp. At the time, trade unionism pretty much looked down on food-related issues, drawing its inspiration from a radical political vision and the messianic ideal of a classless society after the proletariat's ultimate victory. To achieve this dream, one of the absolute, mandatory requirements was the conquest of knowledge. Sembène was among those who were of the persuasion that it is impossible to change the world without understanding it in the first place, and he acted accordingly. He was drawn to the Communist Party because it was also, for him, a gamble on the future. Through his small everyday actions, he felt that he was acting upon the fate of humanity as a whole. "We were all convinced," remembers Bernard Worms, "that the fate of the world was being played out in France." Such a naiveté, coming from such brilliant minds, is rather startling, isn't it? But it's not at all, if one does *not* project the present back into the past, for it should be remembered that the Red Army almost single-handedly defeated the Nazis in Europe, and consequently Stalin was at the peak of his glory. The "Little Father of the People" was then turning Russia, not long before a backward country, into a world superpower.

In the Harlem of Marseilles, Sembène was also caught in the force field of this heady idealism. Not only was he attending the Party's night schools, but he was also listening to the riveting stories told by sea adventurers—thus staying away from smug intellectuals and their "charmed circles," as Fanon would later put it in *The Wretched of the Earth*. "There were old seamen who had journeyed around the world quite a bit, and they fascinated me because they had the experience I was dying to possess."[7] These seamen had such a hold on the 25-year-old laborer's imagination that even more than three decades later, in 1977, Sembène claimed to be still deeply impressed with their stories. Surely, these tales sounded familiar to the young man who, in Dakar, had also basked in an environment where orality reigned supreme. The tales told by his grandmother Fatou Diodio Sène and during the *kasaag* and *taaxuraan*[8] had already awakened his literary sensibility. Above all, these proletarian longshoremen provided him some glimpses into what could be a virile and adventurous life. "I never tired of listening to these old seamen," he confided, "they were telling me about everything, even about the First Pan-African Congress in 1921 that some of them had attended."[9] Sembène is referring here to the *real* First Pan-African Congress held in Paris on February 19–21, 1919—and not in 1921, as he stated. The meeting was initiated by W. E. B. DuBois, with the alleged support of Blaise Diagne, the first Black representative in the French parliament. The organization of this landmark congress was due, to a great extent, to contingent factors, as DuBois was then representing NAACP in Paris, on the occasion of a peace conference.[10] In any event, it was the first concerted reaction of Africans, including those from the diaspora, to the scandalous slicing up of the continent during the 1884–1885 Berlin Conference. At the closing of this First Pan-African Congress, a petition was written, addressed to the Society of Nations, in which were reiterated the right to education for all Black children and the need to "establish a code of laws for the international protection of the natives of Africa"—including land rights, suppression of forced labor, and so forth.

Sembène was also indebted to these old sea rovers in another respect: they introduced him to the works of African American writers who had come to Marseilles in the early twentieth century. "It was from them I first heard the name of the man who wrote *Banjo*, Claude McKay. They had known him personally." Born in 1889 to a family of Jamaican peasants, Claude McKay was, like Sembène, fortunate enough to have attended primary school in his early years. In 1912, he migrated to the United States, where he first encountered racism. In 1913–14, he attended Kansas State University. From 1919 to 1920, during a stay in London, McKay discovered the writings of Marx, and in 1922, after his conversion to communism, he made a trip to the Soviet Union. The following year, and up until 1933, McKay lived in Europe. *Banjo* is, as its subtitle indicates, "a story without a plot," where everything is centered around McKay's experience of Marseilles. Written in 1929, the novel tells the story of its eponymous hero, Banjo, a Black musician, and of his bohemian clique in the underworld of Marseilles in the 1920s. It was through McKay and *Banjo*, which was actually one of the first novels about the Black experience in France, that Sembène discovered the precursors of West Indian literary and political movements, most notably Marcus Garvey's short-lived UNIA and Back-to-Africa project. McKay's novel certainly provided a sort of template for Sembène's own *Black Docker*, for the latter, in his own way, sketches a portrait of the same "milieu" and the same underclass of Black immigrants.

Many events in Sembène's life have aroused and sustained his passion for writing. One of them deserves particular attention here: it was his 1951 work accident, at the *Quai de la Joliette*. With a broken backbone, Sembène had to convalesce for one full year. But after recovering from the accident, he was no longer fit to work and make the descent into ship holds. According to Carrie Moore, that year of physical and spiritual rest gave Sembène the opportunity to reflect on his life as a docker and on the options available to him. As the old saying goes, every cloud has a silver lining, for this accident also provided him with a way out of his dead-end situation as a docker. He certainly did not regret it, judging from the disgust with which his condition filled him. The description of winter, in *Black Docker,* gives some hints of those moments when Sembène was weighed down by a kind of "spleen" of Marseilles:

> But in winter, early fruit and vegetables from Algeria were plentiful. It was a godsend for the dockers. The pace of work exhausted Diaw Falla, his mind was growing feeble. He fled the company of his comrades, and took refuge in silence. He struggled against himself, to stop himself from sinking in what he called "the degeneracy of the times."[11]

Like Diaw Falla, Sembène "had the choice between two personalities: the docker, who was just an animal being, but who lived and paid his rent, or the intellectual who could only survive in a climate of rest and freedom of thought. . . . He spent hours thinking in front of a sheet of paper . . . he was filled with disgust for his profession and began wondering if he could find something else."[12] Back in Marseilles, after his convalescence in Denmark, Sembène found another job as a switchman, thanks to his comrades from CGT. It was far less exhausting than the work of *portefaix*[13] he was holding before the accident.

Even though being a docker, according to Sembène, can only lead one to a dead end, it was also a survival strategy through which he learned to struggle and cope with his hard fate. Writing was a way of escaping a mediocre existence. "I've told you before," yells Diaw Falla at his lover Catherine, "and I'll say it again. I can't get married while I'm a docker. That's no profession. How and where would we live? A hand to mouth existence in a hotel room? No, I don't want that. . . . How many do you know who live in hovels in the most appalling conditions, and blame the whole society? That kind of life is not for me."[14] To rise above his condition, he had to read and read more. At the Communist Party's library, he came across the works of Jack London, one of the greatest socialist writers of the twentieth century. Actually, Sembène had started delving into London's narrative world long before the accident that would cause him to be exonerated from toiling in the holds: "Thanks to my political training, I had a bird's-eye view on society, and this enabled me to do a close-reading of every text. . . . When I was interested in a book, I tried to peel it off, layer after layer, to see what I could keep for my personal benefit."[15] According to Sembène, the encounter with Jack London, through the latter's books, played such an influential role in his decision to become a writer, that it impelled his career and fueled his artistic sensibility. The first great American socialist novelist could only appeal to him, as the unique itinerary of the man who wrote *Martin Eden* foreshadowed Sembène's very own.

John Griffith London was born in San Francisco in 1876, fourteen years before the closing of the Frontier. He died in 1916, one year before the United States involvement in World War I. One could indeed argue that Jack London straddled two epochs, with one foot in the past and another in the future. Of working-class origins, he was situated at a major phase of cultural transition in American society: London was associated with both of the marginalized groups, the proletariat and the upper middle-class. A socialist militant turned writer, London left behind him a mammoth corpus of 41 published novels, hundreds of articles, and thousands of letters. In addition to his literary success, he is today hailed as "the last writer who celebrated the American frontier and the first who sounded the clarion call of battles on the front of social justice."[16] One of the few best-selling authors of his time, London attracted much media attention after making his unusual way to literary fame by slashing through the jungle of poverty and delinquency. In a sense, he was the ideal master for Sembène, the only one who could teach him the art of twisting Fate's arm and of self-improvement through writing.

As evidenced by *Martin Eden,* an autobiographical novel published in 1909,[17] Jack London came to writing in an effort to escape from wretched living conditions. An adventurous, quarrelsome, and rebellious spirit, London, like the novel's eponymous character, did not graduate from high school. According to him, school only offered a drab worldview, it was "not live enough; a passionless pursuit of passionless intelligence." London spent most of his teenage years on the docksides of the Oakland harbor, where he performed all kinds of petty tasks, including some stints as a laborer and factory worker. At some point London was also a railroad worker, and he even became a gold digger in Klondike during the Gold Rush. He moved in the shady circles of oyster pirates and outlaws and was once jailed in New York for vagrancy. But London was also a teenager with an insatiable curiosity, who assiduously visited the municipal libraries in San Francisco and Oakland. Adventure novels soon sparkled his imagination, and like his fictional heroes, London could not resist "the call of the wild" and longed to set out on a sea journey. At only 15, he bought his first craft and started sailing around the San Francisco Bay Area, then all over the American coasts and the five oceans. Although he discovered socialism at 19, his subsequent political beliefs sprang from these life experiences. But for this young man coming from the urban lumpen proletariat, the "people of the abyss,"[18] that encounter with socialism was like a revelation, a dazzling new light; what is more, it beckoned him to an ideal, a noble cause, ultimately instilling in him the firm belief that man can indeed change the course of his life and that of history. London adhered to the Socialist Labor Party in 1896, and eventually became one of the most radical leaders of the American working class. He also took an active part in the suffragette movement. This last point is a crucial one, for the issue of gender equality is also central to Sembène's work, as can be seen in his last two movies, *Faat Kiné* and *Moolaade*. Moreover, Jack London valued art and literature more than "direct" political action. Sembène seems to have heeded this lesson: "For me, there is no better night school than cinema," as he often put it.[19]

Martin Eden, grounded in the experience of proletarian struggles, is the novel that had the deepest and most abiding influence on Sembène. In this text, it gradually becomes clear that for the working class, the only valid art is the one that is created, as London put it later in *The Road,*

> not upon a theme selected from the plenitude of [the artist's] own imagination, but upon the theme he reads in the face of the person who opens the door, be it man, woman, or child, sweet or crabbed, generous or miserly, good-natured or cantankerous, Jew or Gentile, black or white, race-prejudiced or brotherly, provincial or universal, or whatever else it may be.[20]

To put it differently, there is no art but one embedded in a lived reality. It should be added that London's literary models, from whom Sembène also learned a great deal, includes Charles Dickens, Frank Norris, Edgar Allan Poe, Paul Bourget, Victor Hugo, and Jean-Jacques Rousseau. The early works were mostly influenced by Rudyard Kipling, and their thick naturalist veneer earned him a success comparable to Emile Zola's in France. London refined his craft through Zola, who, after a brief flirt with Victor Hugo and Alfred de Musset, had embraced realism. For Zola, a realist novel gave a more faithful picture of society, in spite of the limitations inhering in human sensory and mental perception. The novelist had found in Claude Bernard's experimental biology models that could be applied to the study of society and the human mind. According to Zola, since social environment and heredity are determining each individual's behavior, a novelist must be able to marshal every piece of knowledge he can avail himself of for the study of man. This approach leaves ethical issues on the sidelines, placing greater emphasis on scientific neutrality. Zola's naturalism convinced London that a work of art must be a "document," based on actual reality and wrought from facts one had experienced firsthand. From these two "better craftsmen," Sembène learned that only through a dedicated and painstaking work can one stay in contact with reality. One must be able to gather details and other small pieces of information through minute and relentless research: "I had to get up at 5 and stay up until late in the night; but I was willing to make the sacrifice, because I wanted to express myself."[21] Further, Jack London helped him go beyond naturalism and see in literature a means of transforming social reality and relations. In *Martin Eden,* as in *Black Docker,* a proletarian is seeking salvation through literature.

Later in his life, Sembène would confess: "I came to literature like a blind man recovering his eyesight one fine morning."[22] And one day, during one very relaxed "informal talk" in Rabat, Sembène confided to me that I could write about him with any authority *only* after reading Jack London. Coming from a man who has always been wary of so-called role-models and who has always been reluctant to talk about his influences, such a statement was quite unexpected. He recommended "above all, his biography,"[23] and concluded, musingly: "I was a docker and I dreamed of leading another life. After reading London, I said to myself, 'If this guy has been able, at that time, to beat all the odds, then I can also do it.'"[24] Unfortunately, there were few books on Africa in the Party's library. But Sembène had come across and read Richard Wright's *Native Son:* "This book was perhaps somewhere in the back of my mind while I was writing *Black Docker,* but I didn't agree with Wright, I didn't like the way he portrayed Black people; under his pen they had no consciousness, they just cloaked themselves in their Blackness and aped whites."[25] While dismissing Wright's offhand treatment of the Black question, Sembène admits he was particularly interested in his exploration of racism—a theme he also engages with in *Black Docker.*

Through the Party's school, Sembène came in contact with other progressive writers, although they were less influential. Classes were centered on the applicability of Marxist theory to literature, and Sembène would draw upon them for certain introspective moments in *Black Docker:*

[Diaw] envied his heroes; he could starve them and make them suffer, when he had a full stomach. But now he knew that life was a daily struggle. He learned to loathe the poets and painters who depicted only beauty, who celebrated the glory of spring, forgetting the bitterness of the cold. The birds aren't just decorative, neither are the flowers.[26]

Sembène would have also found the same reflections on the relation between art and politics in the writings of other contemporary authors: John Dos Passos, André Malraux—to whom he sent the manuscript of *God's Bits of Wood*—, Louis-Ferdinand Céline, Ernest Hemingway, and Langston Hughes. "Of course, I started from the bottom up. I eagerly read scores of authors, mostly the French and the Russians. It's very hard to tell who influenced me most, but I spent hours reading them and studying their narrative techniques. . . . Anyway, at the time it was hard for someone who wasn't moving in literary circles to write a book."[27] Among his other formative influences, one could cite the communist Turkish poet Nazim Hikmet, Fyodor Dostoevsky, and Albert Camus.

At the Party's school, literary studies did not boil down to mere "passive" reading; a good deal of the assignments consisted in critical exegeses. Thus, when Sembène finished reading Malraux's *The Human Condition*, he also devoured all the secondary literature on the book, including critical pieces by Stalin and Trotsky.[28] He also knew by heart and often recited Paul Eluard's and Nazim Hikmet's poems. But Sembène did not rest content with simply drugging himself with the contents of these literary and cultural phials, he also appropriated them for his own sake, as shown by "Liberté," his first poem published in *L'Action poétique* in 1956:

I pay tribute
To the ancient Chinese poets
To the Greek philosophers of Antiquity
To the monuments of ancient India
To the strength and fieriness
Of the mobilized Viet Minh people
To the great Antar, a grain of sand
In the ocean of his bled[29] . . .
I admire and envy,
The force of will and love of Russians
For their country, their faith in art.[30]

In spite of this symbiosis between ideas and cultures, and notwithstanding his faith in the redemptive power of art, Sembène could not help sensing something like a huge void, a terrible silence: nowhere was he hearing the voice of his native Africa. In those libraries filled with so many revolutionary works, he saw no trace of a book on Africa, especially his Africa: that of workers and marginalized peoples. This is why he had to fall back on writers from the Black diaspora. By necessity then, Sembène delved deeper into the works of Richard Wright and Claude McKay, but this never brought him to the point of buying into the rhetoric of race as the sole basis for solidarity between Blacks from Africa and the Americas. In this respect, it is worth bearing in mind these two statements made on different occasions: "Mine is a class struggle" (Ouagadougou, 1972) and "My solidarity is not based upon race" (Smith College, 1990). In his reply to Carrie Moore's question concerning a possible union between Blacks from Africa and those from the diaspora, one can clearly see that these ideas had been long brewing and taking shape in his mind:

> Unity for the sake of unity, that won't work for me. This is forced marriage, and it soon ends with a divorce. Why must there be, at any cost, a union between African-Americans and Africans? An African capitalist and an American capitalist get along very well. An African militant and an American militant can similarly be on the same wavelength. Such an alliance would have to proceed along these political lines. . . . To me, solidarity between Blacks is a matter of course, for we have a common denominator, which is colonial oppression. But the situations are quite different. . . . We should avoid falling into the trap of cheap sensationalism.[31]

Ousmane Sembène had an awareness of himself *first* as a docker, *then* as a Black man. All the major decisions he had to make in the course of his life were dictated by class solidarity, which alone was underlying his support to FLN in Algeria and the Viet Minh. It is also on account of these class considerations that he still does not want to claim racial solidarity with *all* African Americans.

Africa has always been foremost among Sembène's concerns during his years of militancy in political parties along with community and student organizations, most particularly after he joined FEANF. He learned much from his interactions, within those militant circles, with intellectuals from France and other parts of the world. But he was never blind to the most essential issue, as he reminds us in the following question: "How could I apply what I learned from progressive artists and men of culture from all around the world, to the case of Africa?" Although he wanted to become a writer for the reason we have already mentioned, namely, to escape his situation as a docker, life also taught him that the priority, for every colonized African, was the liberation of his country. This implied, from his perspective, taking part in the people's struggle for national independence and social revolution.

As early as the 1920s, many African writers had settled in France, a couple of years after the first student contingents had arrived in the metropole. On their way to Paris, these students often passed through Marseilles, which was, as Sembène put it, a kind of "gateway to Africa." In the Latin Quarter, strong ties were established between them and their Black colleagues from the Americas. Over the years, they would attempt, through and beyond their respective organizations, to create common platforms so as to claim or reclaim their common Black heritage. Such was the case in 1934 with the seminal review *L'Etudiant Noir,* and then in 1947 with *Présence Africaine.* Ousmane Sembène was not in direct contact with these Parisian circles, but as an active member of FEANF, he was following their activities with keen interest. Moreover, Sembène had read most of the pioneering texts from the early, interwar period. Besides, writers like Amadou Ndiaye Dugay Clédor (1886–1937), Amadou Mapathé Diagne (1890–1976), Bakary Diallo (1892–1980), and Ousmane Socé Diop (1911–1961) were all from Senegal, like Sembène. The same holds true, of course, for Léopold Sédar Senghor (1906–2002), Abdoulaye Sadji (1910–1961), and Alioune Diop (1910–1966).[32] But Sembène had a particular admiration for Birago Diop (1906–1989), whose folktales revived, according to him, the heartbeats of a people's culture. "The only writer I look upon as a master and a model, when it comes to storytelling, is Birago Diop. I don't know how he sounds in English, but in his case the passage from Wolof to French ran so smoothly, sometimes one feels as if nothing were lost in translation, neither a word, nor even a comma; and all the nuances are there too. That's what I call a master. To the best of my knowledge, he is the only one who has achieved such a feat."[33]

Sembène pronounces a harsh judgment on the literary dynamics of that period: "Initially, African literature wasn't at all oriented toward Africa, it was meant for Europeans, to tell them: 'Look, we have a culture and you still oppress us.' It was what I call a *self-defense literature.* . . . Negritude evolved out of that context: in 1933, it was nothing but the burning desire of some complex-ridden Negroes living in Europe to be accepted by Western culture."[34] However, in spite of this severe critique, Sembène also understood the usefulness of such a literature in a colonial context. Negritude movement writers formed the vanguard in the cultural struggle, and although their texts were written in Europe, and in "foreign" languages to boot, they had a tremendous impact on all Africans: "Even though the African writer couldn't speak directly to his people, echoes of his writings reached Africa, and the latter in return stood by her son. Illiterate people bought the books to have them read in translation by their children. . . . They knew that far away from the continent, their brothers and sisters were standing up for them."[35] This being said, albeit Sembène acknowledges the debt he owes to his literary forebears, the elitist aspects of African literary production in European languages were not lost on him: "I didn't consider myself an artist, but I was constantly telling myself: 'Surely, there should be other means, other ways of voicing the concerns of the people.' . . . I saw people juggling with words and *that* I simply didn't get. I was interested in political issues, not formal researches. On the other hand, you saw people conflating culture with folklore. A culture has nothing whatsoever to do with village dances under the tree. I didn't like that either, but I mostly reproached those writers for their total ignorance of the problems of the masses, especially those of the working class."[36] In the same way he had rejected the assimilationist approach of "mainstream" African politicians, to align himself with the radical theses of Majmout Diop's PAI, Sembène was similarly distancing himself from what he saw as the cultural essentialism of the negritude movement. As far as writers from Africa and the West Indies are concerned, he could relate to the works of Mongo Beti (*Le pauvre Christ de Bomba*, 1956 [as *The Poor Christ of Bomba*, 1971]), Ferdinand Oyono (*Une vie de boy*, 1956), as well as to the penetrating analyses of Césaire, Fanon, Mario de Andrade and, later on, Amilcar Cabral. "I was regularly seeing Mongo Beti, he was in Aix[37] then. Oyono was also in Paris. We formed a small triangle, our books came out in 1956, the same year the International Congress of Black Writers was being held. At the Congress, they didn't want to listen to us, we were seen as 'minors.' We said to them: 'Ok, but we know the future belongs to us.'"[38]

A docker turned writer because he wanted to make himself heard and also deeply resented the elitism of a *certain* African literature, Sembène remained, at 84, a fervent supporter of *Présence Africaine*, the review founded by Alioune Diop in 1947. The two met at the Parisian headquarters of this cultural powerhouse—which by then had also become a high purveyor of francophone literature. They were introduced to Patrice Lumumba at the same time. The Congolese politician was not only an inspirational figure for Sembène, but in a sense it was the journey he made on the Congo River in 1961 that convinced him of the absolute necessity of writing and directing movies. But in spite of his close ties with its founder and director, Sembène found it hard to publish his writings in *Présence Africaine:* "I knew Alioune Diop very well. After the publication of my first poem ["Liberté"] in *Action Poétique,* I tried to have a short-story published in *Présence,* but it was very difficult. Fortunately, Mario de Andrade, the Angolese writer, supported me. If it weren't for him, my text would have been refused."[39] Before gaining prominence as a widely acclaimed writer, Sembène had to "pay his dues" and learn things the hard way, but this was an exciting "personal" struggle for the Black docker in search of his voice—and of an alternative way, too. Speaking of the difficulties encountered while he was writing *Black Docker,* Sembène admitted that he was hugely indebted to Richard Wright: "I wrote *Black Docker* to assert myself. In a sense, I wanted to kill the Father. But I was confronted with serious problems, because I had never before taken up a pen to write a novel. I had no idea how to go about it, I knew that I had to draw upon my own experience, but I spent a heck of a time trying to figure out what story to tell. And while I was grappling with these issues, I had constantly in mind Richard Wright's books."[40] This statement throws light on quite a number of things. One can better see now why the subject matter and even the plot structure of *Black Docker* are modeled upon Wright's *Native Son.* Diaw Falla's is the story of a Black immigrant from Africa who works as a docker in the Marseilles harbor. As in Wright's novel, set in Chicago, the reader in *Black Docker* is presented with a doubly segregated space: Blacks and whites, rich and poor. Like Bigger Thomas, Diaw Falla is both a product and a victim of this type of society, and like Bigger Thomas he accidentally kills a white woman, Ginette Tontisane, a literary go-between who achieves fame by publishing *his* manuscript under *her* own name. In both novels, the trial and conviction following an unpremeditated murder serve as pretexts for a virulent indictment of racial prejudice. Sembène makes no bones about his debt to Wright on all three counts—subject-matter, plot structure, and authorial intent. Like Wright, he also purported to provide a realistic document on the living and working conditions of Black immigrants in France: "The book is partly autobiographical, because some episodes were drawn from my life as a docker and from my daily experiences."[41] *Native Son* was also anchored in the social realism Sembène appreciated so much in Jack London and which was so consonant with his revolutionary ideal: "I need to be in touch with my people. . . . I need to feel the pulses, the smells, I have to witness living scenes; without this raw, tangible material, I can't create anything. . . . We oppressed people, we can't keep silent, that would be a form of collective suicide. If we don't speak out against injustice, we'll be its accomplices."[42] In many respects, *Black Docker* is an artist's attempt to put universal political principles into practice for the sake of African peoples. According to Carrie Moore, the novel is

> *an uneven, loosely structured literary failure. It breaks all rules: unbelievable plot, stereotyped characters, melodramatic tone, and grammatically inaccurate sentences. . . . The work served its purpose in that it represented the conscious effort of a writer to master the word; to pull together a series of experiences around a given theme. . . . This novel [was] somewhat crude in its form.*[43]

Moore clearly failed to grasp the artistic project Sembène was involved in, but this is a point we will not pursue here, as she is anachronistically reading the novel through Arnoldian and Leavisian lenses—but the stiff bowtie of *formal* decorum she is fretting about would still *not* turn Sembène into a Victorian or modernist writer, in whatever "canonical" sense. But Moore also has a strong point: *Black Docker* indeed required from Sembène a quasi superhuman effort to "master the word." It took him two long and consuming years to write, years during which he also had to work to stay alive; not only did he not know how to use a typewriter, but, as indicated in the first edition's dedication ("To Ginette and Odette"), Sembène also needed the patient and loving assistance of his two communist comrades to check the spelling, grammar, and layout. During these 24 months of relentless, intense, and "collaborative" writing,[44] Sembène was deeply obsessed with his book. Every time he visited Odette, he would take with him sheets filled with miscellaneous notes, sketchy sentences, and textual fragments—and everything had to be revised at once!

In spite of all this hassle, the novel was completed in 1955. Then came the harder part: finding a publisher. Présence Africaine refused the manuscript, and like his fictional hero Diaw Falla, the financially beleaguered Sembène had no choice but to publish the novel at his own expense, at Editions Debresse. The first copy was dedicated to Victor Gagnaire, a way for the novelist to express his gratitude to all his comrades in the union and the Party. Sembène once confided to Pierre Haffner, an African film scholar, that his whole life had been an accident. This is a gripping—yet unaffected—and highly accurate formulation. In effect, without his accident Sembène would have probably remained a nobody. After the fracture of his backbone, he was entitled to a pension, but as the payment was slow to materialize, Bernard Worms and other comrades in Marseilles convinced the harbor's administration to consider social reasons so that he could at least be paid a third of his pension.[45] The intervention of his friends enabled Sembène to advance some money to the editor and thus cover part of the publication fees. Three thousand copies were printed for the novel's first edition, which was quickly sold out. It was the griot's voice three thousand times amplified to celebrate the gesta of African peoples fighting for freedom and social justice, a heraldic voice that was already brimming with confidence in "Liberté":

This tom-tom rolling its voice
O plaintive tom-tom!

I pay tribute
To our undivided Africa
To our country, our legends, our myths
This land is ours.
We shall seek its poets,
We shall find its philosophers,
We shall exploit its virgin soil,
We shall erect monuments to honor its heroes,

We shall shape, in the mold of violence, commitment:
A nation.

A tribute to free Africa.[46]

Black Docker was not critically acclaimed, to say the least—not even as a great or "promising" primer. Literary critics in Paris frowned upon it as another anecdotic publication. But in spite of this negative reception, the novel was warmly welcomed by the greater public in Marseilles. In a review published in the communist newspaper *La Marseillaise,* Albert Cervoni writes: "[Ousmane Sembène] has written *Black Docker,* a work that bears testimony to its time, a book whose crafter dipped his pen in the inkwell of exhaustion, hard work and exile blues, and every word bears indelible traces of this."[47] Although Cervoni saw in *Black Docker* a slightly melodramatic novel, he also pointed out that one could sense, beneath the trappings of fiction, a real social drama. The novel tells the story of "Black immigrants living on Rue des Dominicaines, this ghetto plagued with alcoholism and prostitution. The plot conveys . . . through a trial where police and judicial racism itself is put on trial, a burning desire for equality and justice for the oppressed."[48] Cervoni also hailed a first novel in which certain passages had the brutal bluntness of Zola's *L'Assommoir*. However, he invited his readers to hear, beyond all this vehemence, the passionate protest of a man against a degrading society.

More crucially, *Black Docker* should be viewed as the "birth certificate" of a militant-artist. Sembène had found his voice and his vocation, and now he had only to put himself into the service of Africa. The native land and the "beautiful people" so dear to Oumar Faye were already looming large on the horizon. Arguably, this first novel symbolically mapped out the return path of the prodigal son. Like Manuel in Jacques Roumain's classic novel, the reading of which left him in rapt admiration of the Haitian writer, Sembène dreamed of becoming, in his turn, a "master of the dew."[49] At a deeper level, Sembène's long and productive career as a writer and filmmaker can only be seen in light of this irrepressible desire to speak on behalf of the African people and the whole suffering humanity. This is not an overstatement, for he himself says much in the following lines:

> *I want to be a poet*
> *Only for your sake,*
> *Your only griot.*
> *I only want*
> *To sing the praises of our elders,*
> *To wake you to the sound of my kora,*
> *To partake of your greatness.*[50]

It was this same Promethean desire to recover the silenced voices of history that prompted Sembène to embrace cinema. Given the chronic illiteracy then prevailing in Africa, the move was highly strategic and utterly realistic. Later on, Sembène went to study filmmaking in Russia, at the Gorky Studio in Moscow—with Mark Donskoi as his mentor.[51] Upon completion of his training in 1962, he returned to Senegal, with an old 35 mm camera in his suitcases. Then began a half-century-long film career that Sembène would pursue simultaneously with his literary career.

Ousmane Sembène and Samba Gadjigo, United States, 1989.
Photo courtesy of Thomas Jacob.

Conclusion

We began this study by following the ship bringing Oumar Faye back to his native Casamance in *O pays, mon beau peuple!,* after years of war, exile, and learning in Europe. This foreshadowed Sembène's own return, after Senegal's independence in 1960. Like Oumar Faye, Sembène went back to his native land after twelve years in Marseilles; years of personal struggle, that of the war veteran now engaged in a fight against colonialism and frustrated by his own ignorance. During those formative years, Sembène was to gain a new knowledge and embrace a humanism steeped in Marxist ideology, which would eventually structure his thinking and orient his action. In so doing he was, unawares, forging his own destiny. The conquest of this new knowledge empowered Ousmane Sembène, who emerged from silence and anonymity, and found, through writing, a voice all his own. This Marseilles period was also marked by collective struggles within various political and labor organizations, alongside thousands of men from all countries, all driven and united by the same ideal: that of changing the world and ushering in a new era of equality, justice, and universal brotherhood. Sembène went back to Africa seething with a new passion: to take an active part, through his art, in Senegal's cultural emancipation.

Upon his return to Senegal, Ousmane Sembène ceased all political activities, devoting all his militant energy to filmmaking and literature. From 1960, he published ten novels, including three that he penned while still in Marseilles. A literary œuvre that has not only been a source of inspiration for subsequent generations of writers on the African continent, but has also generated a considerable amount of criticism. Translated into numerous languages,[1] today Sembène's work is taught everywhere in Africa and in the rest of the world.

However, beyond this contribution to African literature, what future generations will learn from Ousmane Sembène is that, above all, he was quick to detect and acknowledge the limitations of the literary medium in a continent where most people were—and still are—unable to read and write, both in African or European languages—and also in Arabic, for that matter. By going back to school in 1942, and by attending a film institute later on at 40, Sembène gave himself the means to open new vistas of cultural expression for artists in his country and Africa.

Although he was not the first African to shoot movies, Sembène remains nevertheless one of the most innovative filmmakers of his generation. In addition to his 1966 *Black Girl,* the first feature film ever released by a director from Sub-Saharan Africa, Sembène broke new ground with the 1968 *Mandabi,* the first movie made in an African language, in this case Wolof. Since then, always anxious to reach a wider public in Africa, Sembène made a movie in Joola (spoken in Senegal) and in Jula (spoken in Burkina-Faso and Mali)—movies that have also reached a large international viewership, through subtitling. In Africa, one simply cannot avoid Sembène's cinematographic work, whether one is an epigone eager to perpetuate tradition or an innovator contesting the master's legacy. Likewise, his work is steadily arousing interest among African literature and film scholars.

In addition to his participation, since the 1956 First International Congress of Black Writers and Artists, in literary and artistic activities, Sembène was also the co-founder of numerous cultural organizations. He took part in all the major cultural events on the continent, whether it was the Journées cinématographiques de Carthage (Carthage International Film Festival), the Semaine du cinéma africain de Ouagadougou (later to become FESPACO), or the First World Festival of Negro Arts, held in Dakar in 1966.

As already pointed out, Sembène's work has attracted much critical interest, but all the studies devoted to it are fragmentary, analytically unfocused, and often "hemiplegic," dealing either with cinema or literature. The present biography is an attempt to synthesize Sembène's life experiences, so as to gain insight into the existential matrix, the genesis of his ideas and works, both literary and cinematic. A recent study by David Murphy, entitled *Ousmane Sembène: Imagining Alternatives in Film and Fiction* (2000), and drawing on the findings of Senegalese historians such as Mamadou Diouf, has shed some light on what seems to be the guiding thread of Sembène's entire œuvre, namely the fact that it is, of necessity, contrapuntal and always countervailing the "official" narratives, whether political or religious. But to date, there is no comprehensive study of Sembène's corpus within a framework large enough to include the various contingencies underlying it. Yet only through such a synthetic, macro-level approach can one bring to light the work's complexity, its thematic and aesthetic consistency, as well as evaluate the scope and limitations of its political resonance.

BIOGRAPHICAL
LANDMARKS

Biography of Ousmane Sembène	Landmark Events
1645	The Portuguese take possession of the area where Ziguinchor is currently located.
1790	The Lebus, Ousmane Sembène's ethnic group, a community of fishermen who came from the Fuuta by way of the Kingdom of Kayor, create the Republic of Cap Vert.
1812 Saër Sembène, Ousmane's paternal grandfather, settles in Mboth, the current site of Dakar Plateau.	Under the leadership of Dial Diop, the Lebus wrest their freedom from the despotic Damel Amari Ngoné Coumba and proclaim the independence of the peninsula.
1814	A treaty signed on May 14 seals France's acquisition of Gorée Island.
1857	On May 25, annexation of Dakar by France, after a successful naval raid on the city launched from the *Jeanne d'Arc*.

1886	Death of Lat-Dior, king of Kayor and last major figure of armed resistance against France.
	"Pacification" of the entire country, with the exception of Casamance.
	France's acquisition of Casamance, through a treaty signed with Portugal.
	The Joola rebellion against the French colonial authority.
	Intensification of peanut farming in Casamance.
1889	Birth of Lamine Senghor—Léopold Sédar Senghor's cousin. Injured during World War I, he settles in Paris and eventually sets up the Defense Committee of the Negro Race. Drawn to Marxism, in 1927 he takes part, in Brussels, in the creation of the League Against Imperialism and Colonial Oppression and is elected to the steering committee. Arrested in 1929, he dies in prison.
1902	Dakar becomes the capital of French West Africa (AOF), replacing Saint-Louis.
1917	Appointment of Senegalese representative Blaise Diagne as General Commissioner of African troops.
	The Joola resistance compels Governor Richard Brunot to contrive a "pacification" plan for Casamance that ends in a bloodbath.
1918	On March 5–6, a visit to Ziguinchor by Blaise Diagne, during a recruiting tour. He is copiously insulted and a young Joola girl slaps him in the face.
1920	Birth of Aliin Sitooye Jaata, the "queen of Kabrousse."
1923 On January 1st, Ousmane Sembène is born in Ziguinchor.	Issuance of a decree outlawing "cannibalism" in French West Africa.

1927	Execution of freedom fighters in Ziguinchor, at the behest of colonial administrator Maubert, allegedly for "cannibalism."
1928	Birth in Oussouye of Abbé Diamacoune Senghor.

1931
Enters primary school at Ecole Escale in Ziguinchor.

1938
Enters 5th grade, with Jean Kandé as teacher, but he is expelled after an altercation with his superintendent, Paul Péraldi.

Starts fishing with his father, Moussa.

Is "transferred" to Dakar. Settles in Plateau, at 45 Rue de Thiong and repeats 5th grade at Ecole de la Rue de Thiong.

Sees a screening of *The Gods of the Stadium,* a documentary movie on the 1936 Munich Olympic Games by Leni Riefenstahl.

1939 Works in Dakar as construction helper for his paternal uncle Baye Wélé Sembène, senior construction worker.	September 1: beginning of WWII. October 15: Open letter by Black representative Galandou Diouf, published in *Paris-Dakar,* exhorting Black fighters to take up arms against Germany.
1940 September 23–25: Sembène witnesses the air raid on Dakar by the Allied Forces. The Lebu settlements in the Plateau are the most affected.	May: start of the German occupation of France. June 18: De Gaulle's resounding call to resistance from the BBC in London.
Joins the Layène brotherhood.	Night raid on Marseilles by Mussolini's forces. July 13: Arrival in Dakar of Vichy-appointed governor Pierre Boisson. September 25: fierce resistance by the Vichy troops impels the Allied Forces to withdraw. Organization by Aliin Sitooye Jaata of the first Joola rebellion against French colonial authorities.

1941

Takes part, as a construction helper, in the building of the Van Vollenhoven high school, under the supervision of Boubacar Diouf "Rafet," senior construction worker at the Pinet Laprade Vocational School.

Creation in France of the National Movement against Racism (MNCR), later to become the Movement against Racism and for Friendship between Peoples (MRAP).

1942

Refusal by Joola farmers to pay the rice tax imposed by the French administration (theme of the 1971 movie *Emitaï*).

1943

Arrest of Aliin Sitooye Jaata, who is sentenced to ten years of exile and prison.

January 16: the Germans blow up the Rue du Vieux Port in Marseilles with dynamite.

1944

On February 1st, Sembène is drafted into the French army. He receives basic training, as Private 689, at Camp Militaire des Mamelles (Dakar military base).

In April, leaves for Niger with the Sixth Colonial Infantry Regiment.

From January 30 to February 8: Brazzaville Conference.

May: Liberation of Marseilles.

August 25: Liberation of Paris.

December 1st: Thiaroye massacre.

1945

Ho Chi Minh's proclamation of independence for the Democratic Republic of Vietnam.

May 8: bloody repression of the Sétif rebellion in Algeria.

1946

Completes compulsory 18-month military service. Returns to Dakar.

Joins the union of construction workers and, for the first time, is involved in militant activities.

Shows first signs of a budding political consciousness.

Breaks with the *Layène* religious brotherhood and regularly attends political rallies organized by Lamine Guèye.

In September, becomes a stowaway on the *Pasteur,* a ship bound for Marseilles.

In January, 14-day strike in Dakar, organized by civil servants and employees in the commerce, industry, and banking sectors (EMCIBA).

The creation, by metal workers and dockers in Dakar, of the Union des syndicats confédérés (Confederation of trade unions), headed by Lamine Diallo.

The transmutation of the French colonial empire into the Union Française.

April 25: loi Lamine Guèye (Lamine Guèye bill) entitles *all* French *subjects* to full citizenship.

Settles for a while on Rue Sylvabelle, in the l'Opéra neighborhood.

Works as a docker at the Quai de la Joliette, in the Vieux-Port (Old Harbor) of Marseilles. Now lives in the African neighborhood, on Rue des Dominicaines.

1947

1948

1950
Joins CGT.

March 10: takes part in an unlimited strike staged by the CGT union of dockers in Marseilles.

1951
A work accident leaves Sembène with a fractured backbone.

After his convalescence, he can no longer descend into the hold and works instead as a switchman.

Joins the French Communist Party (PCF).

Starts regularly visiting CGT libraries and attending PCF's classes. Reads the works of communist writers, discovers communist youth hostels, and is introduced to red dramatics (social protest theater).

Becomes very active in African grassroots organizations.

Starts writing *Black Docker.*

October 18–21: creation in Bamako of the African Democratic Alliance (RDA), then closely affiliated with the French Communist Party (PCF).

From October 10, 1947, to March 19, 1948: legendary strike of the Dakar-Niger railroad workers.

In Paris, founding of *Présence Africaine* by Alioune Diop.

Publication by Léopold Sédar Senghor of *Anthologie nègre et malgache* (Anthology of Negro poetry).

Creation of the Foyer des Africains de Marseille (African association of Marseilles).

Severance by RDA of all ties with PCF, followed by closer attachment to the Union Démocratique et Socialiste de la Résistance (Democratic and socialist union of the resistance), through the workings of François Mitterrand.

1952

Starts participating, as a militant, in all the demonstrations against the Korean War, the Indochina War, and the trial of Ethel and Julius Rosenberg.

1953

Appears as an extra in *Le Rendez-vous des quais,* by communist schoolteacher-turned-director Paul Scarpita.

In June, execution of the Rosenberg couple in New York.

1954

Takes part in all the demonstrations against the colonial war in Algeria.

July 13–21: takes part in the strike against the war in Indochina.

First FLN attacks in Kabylia, on All Saints Day. Start of the Algerian War of Liberation.

1956

Publishes "Liberté," his first poem, in *Action Poétique.*

Publishes at his own expense his first novel, *Black Docker,* at Editions Debresse.

Attends the First International Congress of Black Writers, held in Paris.

Becomes secretary-general of the Organization of Black Workers in France.

Publication by Mongo Beti of *Le pauvre Christ de Bomba* [as The Poor Christ of Bomba, 1971].

Une vie de boy, by Ferdinand Oyono.

June 23: approval by the National Assembly of the loi-cadre Deferre (Deferre framework bill), drafted and proposed by Gaston Deferre, then mayor of Marseilles and Minister of Overseas Colonies. The bill makes it possible to create democratically elected government councils in overseas territories.

1957

Creates in Marseilles a chapter of the African Independence Party (PAI).

Publishes *O pays, mon beau peuple!,* his second novel.

1958

PCF sends him to Prague to complete a one-month training program.

September 28: Referendum in French West Africa on de Gaulle's proposal for a *Communauté Française* (French union). Only Guinea votes no.

October 2: independence of Guinea, under the leadership of Sékou Touré.

1959
Sembène creates in Marseilles a chapter of the African Party for the Independence of Guinea-Bissau and Cape Verde (PAIGC).

Attends the Second International Congress of Black Writers, held in Rome.

In January, creation of the Federation of Mali (Senegal, French Sudan, Haute Volta, and Dahomey); Dahomey and Haute Volta leaves the Federation in March.

August 3: massacre of 50 striking dockers in the Pidjiguti harbor (Guinea-Bissau).

In Bordeaux, after the December 28–30 Congress, creation of the Federation of French West African Students (FEANF).

May 29: creation of the *Conseil de l'Entente* (Ivory Coast, Dahomey, Haute Volta, and Niger).

Creation of the Federation of Mali, comprising only Senegal and French Sudan.

1960
Publishes *Les bouts-de-bois-de-Dieu* [*God's Bits of Wood,* 1962].

Relinquishes his French citizenship, leaves PCF and all other political organizations he was a member of. Returns to Senegal.

August 20: independence of Senegal.

September 22: independence of French Sudan, which becomes the Republic of Mali.

These two independences lead to the collapse of the Federation of Mali.

1961

Assassination of Patrice Lumumba, Prime Minister of Congo.

Creation by Cheikh Diop of BMS (People's movement of Senegal).

1962
The short story collection *Voltaïque, suivi de la Noire de . . .* is published.

Learns filmmaking in Moscow, at the Gorky Studio.

July 3: independence of Algeria.

Imprisonment of ANC leader Nelson Mandela.

Constitutional crisis in Senegal, leading to the imprisonment of Senghor's prime minister Mamadou Dia.

1963
Borom Saret (The horsecart driver), his first short feature, is awarded the prize for best first movie at the Tours Film Festival in France.

Creation of OAU (Organization of African Unity) in Addis-Abeba.

Start of armed struggle for the liberation of Guinea-Bissau.

Second Republic in Senegal.

1964

The novel *L'harmattan* is published.

Releases *Niaye,* a short feature. Wins the CIC Prize at the Tours Film Festival; receives a special mention at the Locarno Film Festival in Switzerland.

1966

Vehi Ciosane, suivi du Mandat (*White Genesis, with The Money Order,* 1972).

Releases *Black Girl,* his first long feature. Wins numerous prizes, including the prize for best movie at the First World Festival of Negro Arts and *Tanit d'or* at the Carthage International Film Festival.

Wins First Literary Prize at the First World Festival of Negro Arts.

1967

Is a member of the jury at the Cannes Film Festival.

1968

Releases *Mandabi* (The money order), long feature. The movie wins the Jury Prize at the Venice film festival; and the First Prize at the Philadelphia Black Film Festival, USA, 1973.

Is Jury President at the Carthage International Film Festival.

1969

Directs a short feature, *Traumatisme de la femme face à la polygamie* (Trauma of women facing polygamy) for French public television.

Directs *Les dérives du chômage* (The perils of unemployment) for French public television.

Co-founder of the Semaine du cinéma de Ouagadougou (African Film Week, later to be renamed FESPACO, the Ouagadougou International Film Festival).

Dissolution of PRA (Party of African unity) into Senghor's UPS (Progressive union of Senegal).

First World Festival of Negro Arts in Dakar.

Creation, in Tunisia, of the Carthage International Film Festival.

Presidential election in Senegal. Senghor is the only candidate.

In May, students at the university of Dakar and high schoolers all over Senegal go on strike.

General strike staged by the National union of workers (UNTS).

Student strike in Dakar; the university is closed.

Declaration by the Senegalese government of a state of emergency.

Creation of the National confederation of workers (CNTS), replacing UNTS.

First Semaine du cinéma africain de Ouagadougou.

Creation of FEPACI (Pan-African Federation of Film Professionals).

Co-founder of FEPACI (Pan-African Federation of Film Professionals).

1970

1971
Receives the Afro-Asian Literary Prize (Lotus Prize, Cairo, Egypt).

Is a correspondent member of the Academy of Letters (Republic of Germany).

Releases *Taaw* (The firstborn), a short feature. Wins the Asmara Gold Lion (Ethiopia).

Releases *Emitaï*, a long feature. Wins the Silver Bear at the Berlin Film Festival; the 2nd prize at the Moscow Film Festival; and the First Afro-Asian Prize at the Tachkent Film Festival (Soviet Union).

1972
Directs a short feature, *Basket Africain aux Jeux Olympiques de Munich* (African basketball at the Munich Olympic Games).

1973
Publishes *Xala,* a novel (as *Xala,* 1976). Directs *L'Afrique aux Olympiades* (Africa at the Olympics), a short feature.

1974
Releases *Xala,* a long feature. Wins the Karlovy-Vary Special Prize (Czechoslovakia).

Pan-African Cultural Manifesto, also known as the Algiers Cultural Charter.

Start of Biafra civil war in Nigeria.

Death of Gamal Abdel Nasser.

Constitutional reform in Senegal: Senghor appoints Abdou Diouf as prime minister.

Open rejection by Senegalese farmers of the policies of ONCAD (National organization of development centers) and refusal to grow peanuts.

Visit to Senegal by French president Georges Pompidou.

Student strike in Senegal. Arrest and deportation of the leaders.

In Senegal, creation of National Society of Cinematography (SNC).

The Semaine du cinéma africain becomes FESPACO.

Assassination of Amilcar Cabral in Guinea-Bissau.

In Senegal, creation of SIDEC, a state-owned company regulating the exploitation and distribution of local and foreign films.

In Ethiopia, fall of Haile Selassie's regime.

Independence gained by former Portuguese colonies (Guinea-Bissau, Angola, Mozambique, and Cape Verde).

General amnesty for political prisoners in Senegal, including Mamadou Dia and Majmout Diop.

Creation by Abdoulaye Wade of PDS (Democratic party of Senegal).

1975
Is a member of the jury at the Moscow Festival.

Creation of ECOWAS (Economic organization of West African states).

1976
Releases *Ceddo,* a long feature. Wins the Special Prize at the Los Angeles Film Festival.

Soweto uprising in apartheid South Africa.

Replacement of UPS (Progressive union of Senegal) by PS (Socialist party).

Constitutional reform in Senegal, paving the way for three official political parties: PS, PDS, and PAI.

1977
Honored on the occasion of the 60th anniversary of Soviet cinema.

Second World Festival of Negro Arts, held in Lagos (Nigeria).

Is jury president at the Berlin Film Festival.

1980

Announcement by Senghor in Senegal of his resignation from the presidency, on New Year's Eve.

1981
Publishes *Le dernier de l'Empire* (The Last of the Empire: A Senegalese Novel, 1983).

January 1: Abdou Diouf the new president of Senegal.

Forcing by IMF of its SAP (Structural Adjustment Plan) on the newly formed government.

Is jury president at the New Delhi Film Festival.

Creation of the Confederation of Senegambia, with Abdou Diouf as president and Dawda Jawara as vice-president.

Is jury president at the Pan-African Film Festival in Ouagadougou (FESPACO).

1982

Launch of first guerilla raids on the Senegalese army by MFDC, under Abbé Diamacoune's leadership.

1983
Is a member of the jury at the Mostra (Venice Film Festival).

Induction of Senghor into the French Academy.

1984
Is a member of the jury at the Rio de Janeiro Film Festival.

Death of Sékou Touré in the U.S.

In Senegal, creation of SNPC (New company for the promotion of cinema).

1986

Death of Cheikh Anta Diop; the University of Dakar is renamed after him.

1987
Publishes *Niiwam* (*Niiwaam and Taw: Two Novellas*, 1992).

Honored at the Festival of Non-Aligned and Developing Countries (Pyong-Yang, North Korea).

1988
Releases *Camp de Thiaroye,* a long feature. Wins five awards at the 45th Venice Film Festival:

In February, presidential election in Senegal. Opposition parties protest against election rigging. Diouf declares a state of emergency and has all opposition leaders jailed.

Jury's Special Grand Prize

UNICEF Award

Cinema Nuovo Award

Youth and Cinema Award

Golden Ciak Award

Also wins Jury's Special Prize at the Carthage Film Festival and the OAU Prize.

1989
Camp de Thiaroye wins Black Peoples Award at FESPACO.

In April, political tensions between Senegal and Mauritania.

In September, dissolution of Confederation of Senegambia.

1990
Is a member of the jury at the World Encounters Film Festival (Finland).

Liberation of Nelson Mandela.

First edition of RECIDAK (Dakar Film Festival).

1991
Receives the African Creativity Award at FESPACO.

Opposition leader Abdoulaye Wade's integration of the government as State Minister (without any specific policy). Short-lived cohabitation with Abdou Diouf.

1992
Releases *Guelwaar,* a long feature.

Is jury president at the Carthage Film Festival.

Receives the Living Legend Award at the National Black Arts Festival in Atlanta.

1993
Is co-recipient of Grand Prix de la République du Sénégal pour les Arts et les Lettres.

Assassination of Justice Boubacar Sèye, vice-president of the Constitutional Council in Senegal.

For his 30 years of cinema, Sembène is honored by the Ministry of Culture in Burkina Faso and the secretary-general of FEPACI.

1994

End of apartheid in South Africa. Mandela is elected president.

Currency depreciation in French-speaking Africa.

1995

Celebration of African cinema's 50th anniversary.

1996
Publishes *Guelwaar,* a novel.

Creation in Senegal, of a 60-member senate by Abdou Diouf.

1999
Releases a short feature, *Héroïsme au quotidien* (Everyday heroism).

Abdoulaye Wade's one-year self-imposed exile in France.

2000
Releases *Faat Kine,* a long feature.

February 27: PDS presidential election winning; Abdoulaye Wade becomes the third president of Senegal.

2001

Creation of the African Union, replacing former OAU.

In March, Mame Madior the first female prime minister in Senegal.

2004
Releases *Moolaade,* a long feature. Wins *Un Certain Regard* Prize at Cannes (unofficial Palme d'Or for movies not competing in the official selection); receives Special Award at the Chicago Film Festival.

2005
Receives the *Carrosse d'or* (Golden coach) at Cannes.

Ellen Johson-Sirleaf, the first female president in Liberia.

Selected to give a movie lesson at Cannes.

Moolaade wins Health Ministry Prize (Burkina Faso) at FESPACO.

2006
Senegalese government declares Sembène a *Trésor humain vivant* (Living human treasure).

Is awarded the *Légion d'honneur* by the French Republic.

2007
ECOBANK creates an Ousmane Sembène Award at the 20th FESPACO.

June 9: Ousmane Sembène dies in Dakar.

French president Jacques Chirac's visit to Senegal.

Death of Majmout Diop.

Death of Abbé Diamacoune Senghor.

Re-election of Abdoulaye Wade as president for a five-year term.

NOTES

Preface

1. André Lagarde, Laurent Michard, Collection "Textes et Littérature," in collaboration with Raoul Audibert, Henri Lemaitre, and Thérèse Van Der Elst (Paris: Bordas, 1964).

2. *Changer la vie* (To change life), the students' slogan, taken from Rimbaud's *A Season in Hell,* was of course resonant with Marxist overtones.

3. Frantz Fanon, *Les damnés de la terre,* preface by Jean-Paul Sartre, 2nd ed. (Paris: Maspéro, 1961); translated by Constance Farrington as *The Wretched of the Earth* (New York: Grove Press, 1965).

4. Ousmane Sembène, *Les bouts de bois de dieu* (Paris: Le livre contemporain, 1960); translated by Ros Schwartz as *God's Bits of Wood* (London: Heinemann, 1962).

5. Paulin Soumanou Vieyra, *Ousmane Sembène, cinéaste, la première période, 1962–1971* (Paris: Présence Africaine, 1972). Along with Sembène, Vieyra, born in Benin and a Senegalese by adoption, is among the pioneers of African cinema. His 1955 short feature, *Afrique-sur-Seine,* about the African diaspora in Paris, is widely regarded as the first movie made by a director from Sub-Saharan Africa. In 1973

he wrote the first book on the history of African cinema and, more importantly, produced many of Sembène's early movies, including *Emitaï* and *Xala*. He also mentored the Bissau-Guinean director Flora Gomes. He died in 1987 in Paris, at the age of 62.

6. Birago Diop, *La plume raboutée: Mémoires* (Paris: Présence Africaine, 1978).

Part 1. On the Banks of a Mighty River

T.N.: Unless otherwise credited, all quotes are newly translated from the French source text.

The epigraph is from Ousmane Sembène, *O pays, mon beau peuple!* (Paris: Presses Pocket, 1957).

1. Casamance

1. Ousmane Sembène, *Archives sonores de la littérature africaine,* presented by Jacques Howlett (Paris: Clef, n.d.). This audio document should be a mandatory starting point for any researcher who wants to undertake an in-depth study of Sembène's life and work.

2. *Séléki* also refers both to an ethnic group and to a former kingdom in Casamance. The area was a stronghold of resistance against French penetration into the region, and on December 1, 1886, the natives fought the French in the so-called Séléki Battle. Although the battle was lost, they also caused heavy casualties among the invaders.

3. On May 17, 1906, Djignabo Badji led the attack against the French. Badji was a charismatic spiritual leader who attended to the fetishes (*bëkin*) in Séléki and was consequently reputed to be invulnerable. As can be expected, his death at the hands of the French has given rise to numerous legends, which eventually became part of the revolutionary lore in this region.

4. Sembène, *Archives sonores.*

5. *Emitaï,* 1971, feature film, 16 mm, color, 101 min. This is Sembène's first historical movie and is devoted to the confrontation between the French colonial authority and the Joola community of Casamance during World War II. The movie is largely inspired by the epic resistance Aliin Sitooye Jaata organized during the forties. Charged with inciting a rebellion, Jaata was deported to Kayes, in Mali, and later to Timbuktu in 1943, where she eventually died in 1947.

6. Djib Diédhiou, "An Interview with Ousmane Sembène," *Le Soleil,* November 7, 1993, pp. 8–9.

7. For more on the historical specificity of the *quatre communes,* see François Zuccarelli, *La vie politique dans les quatre communes du Sénégal de 1871 à 1914* (Ph.D. diss., Université de Paris I, 1970).

8. *Indigénat* is an administrative regime typical of colonial management in the French style. It is a system in which the natives are subjected to a discriminatory and disenfranchising legal code, the infamous *code de l'indigénat,* which was first introduced in Algeria in 1881.

9. Suppletory judgments could only be issued to educated natives whose status as civil servants involved frequent interactions with the French administration.

10. Informal talk with Ousmane Sembène. I will use this expression throughout. Rather than "interview," "talk" seems a more apt formulation, for these conversations I had with Sembène were not scheduled beforehand, let alone recorded; they took place randomly, and the notes I have taken of Sembène's words do not fit into the traditional Q&A format of interviews. These talks were the only moments with him when I could catch a glimpse into the formative events of his life. The difficulty resides in the fact that Sembène often switches to another subject whenever he feels that he is being prodded into taking a given path. These informal talks, although at times frustrating, have been more rewarding for me than the regular Q&A sessions during which Sembène often "dribbles" his interlocutors with a disconcerting ease.

11. Religious brotherhood founded by Seydina Limamou Laye (1843–1949). It is the third largest brotherhood after the Murids and the Tijaans.

12. Jacqueline Trincaz, *Colonisations et religions en Afrique noire: l'exemple de Ziguinchor,* preface by Louis-Vincent Thomas (Paris: L'Harmattan, 1981), p. 26.

13. The exciting prospects for research should be a strong incentive for young scholars.

14. Ibid., p. 9.

15. On Senegambia, see Laurent Jean Baptiste and Bérenger-Féraud, *Les peuplades de la Sénégambie: histoire, ethnographie, m œurs et coutumes, légendes, etc.* (Paris: E. Leroux, 1879). See also Boubacar Barry, *La Sénégambie du XVᵉ au XIXᵉ siècle: Traite négrière, Islam et conquête coloniale* (Paris: L'Harmattan, 1991).

16. Abbé Augustin Diamacoune Senghor (1928–2007), who was successively incarcerated from 1982 to 1987 and from 1990 to 1991, was the leader of the secessionist movement in Casamance. The MFDC, created in 1947 by Senghor, would eventually become an underground movement after a peaceful demonstration in Ziguinchor, held on December 26, 1982, was harshly repressed. Senghor died on January 17, 2007. MFDC continues to be the main secessionist movement in Casamance.

17. *Ceddo* designates a community whose visceral attachment to its own totemic practices and fierce opposition to Islamization, Christianization, and colonization, set its members apart in Senegalese society.

2. At the Crossroads of Cultures

1. Ousmane Sembène, *Archives sonores.*

2. The Baïnouks are the oldest community in Senegal. At the time of the Mali empire, during the thirteenth century, they lived further north, in the Sine and Saloum regions. Although they were eventually forced to move south by the Serers and the Mandingos, they have always enjoyed the protection of the latter, who ruled over southern Senegal and had founded the Kaabu kingdom. Owing to their minority status, they could not hold sway over the other populations, let alone create any kingdom. They could only establish small chieftaincies scattered over the region.

3. Sembène, *Archives sonores.*

4. For more on Futa Toro, see James P. Johnson, "The Almamate of Futa Toro, 1779–1836: A Political History" (Ph.D. diss., University of Wisconsin, Madison, 1974); Mouhamed Moustapha Kane, "A History of Fuuta Tooro, 1890s–1920s: Senegal under Colonial Rule" (Ph.D. diss., Michigan State University, East Lansing, 1987); David Wallace Robinson Jr., "Abdul Bokar Kan and the History of Futa Toro: 1853 to 1891" (Ph.D. diss., Columbia University, New York, 1971).

5. Sembène, *Archives sonores.*

6. Sembène, *O pays,* p. 32.

7. Ibid., p. 60.

8. Marie Dia, interview with the author, Ziguinchor, 1997.

9. Souleymane Ndiaye Dimitri, interview with the author, Ziguinchor, 1997.

10. Ousmane Sembène, informal talk with the author, Yoff, 1999.

11. It is worth noting that although a Lebu by birth, Sembène is, from a wider cultural perspective, a "dyed-in-the-wool Joola."

12. Kahone had been the capital city of the Sine Saloum kingdom since the fifteenth century, before gradually losing its prominence under the French rule, as colonial administration concentrated its activities around Kaolack. Today Kahone is a major pilgrimage site for practitioners of traditional religion in the Sine Saloum region. Every year they hold the famous *gamou,* a communal event which goes back to the sixteenth century and involves ritual dances with masks and divination practices to predict the beginning and end of the rainy season.

13. The *tuur* is a totemic animal representing the tutelary ancestors.

3. Youth and Its Discontents

1. Sembène, *Archives sonores.*

2. Sembène, *O pays,* p. 98.

3. Sembène, *Archives sonores.*

4. Ibid.

5. Sembène, *O pays,* p. 108.

6. Ibid., p. 18.

7. Ousmane Sembène, *Faat Kiné,* feature film, 102 min., Filmii Doomireew, 2000. This is the second movie in Sembène's three-part series on the everyday heroism of ordinary people, especially Senegalese and African women, a trilogy comprising *L'héroïsme au quotidien* (1999) and *Moolaade* (2004).

8. Sembène, *O pays,* p. 116.

9. This theme of the "return to the native land" is also taken up in *Guelwaar* (see n. 21, below) (Barthélemy) and *Faat Kiné* (Djib).

10. According to Moussa Barro, Ousmane was so reserved that his schoolmates called him a "savage." Interestingly enough, Boubacar Boris Diop uses the same adjective to describe the look Sembène is casting on Senegalese society.

11. Vieyra, *Ousmane Sembène cineaste.*

12. Sembène, *O pays,* pp. 36–37.

13. Statements reported to me by Ousmane Sembène during an informal talk held in July 1997.

14. Marie Dia, interview with the author, Ziguinchor, 1997.

15. T.N.: *Marabouts* in this case are traditional healers with a sound knowledge of both the Koran and of indigenous healing practices. They should be confused neither with Arabic school teachers, nor with community spiritual leaders, both also called *marabout* or *seriñ* (guides).

16. Statements reported to me by Ousmane Sembène during an informal talk held in July 1997.

17. Marsassoum is a small rural settlement on the banks of the Soungrougrou River, 33 km from Ziguinchor.

18. Carrie Dailey Moore, *Evolution of an African Artist: Social Realism in the Works of Ousmane Sembène* (Ann Arbor, Mich.: University Microfilms, 1973).

19. Ousmane Sembène, informal talk with the author, Yoff, 1999.

20. Ibid.

21. Ousmane Sembène, *Guelwaar,* co-produced by Filmii Doomireew and Galaté Film, 1993.

22. Sembène, *Archives sonores.*

23. Ousmane Sembène, informal talk with the author, Yoff, 1999.

24. Ousmane Sembène, interview given to Houston Public Television, Texas, 1996.

25. I tried to interview Jacques Perrin after he went back to France, but at the mere mention of the name "Sembène," he hung up the phone, which suggests that it would have been too masochistic on his part to evoke memories of this collaboration.

26. Ousmane Sembène, informal talk with the author, Yoff, 1999.

27. Marie Dia, interview with the author, Ziguinchor, 1996.

28. Ousmane Sembène, informal talk with the author, Yoff, 1999.

29. Ibid.

30. Ibid.

31. Camara Laye, *Dark Child* (New York: Noonday Press, 1994).

32. Mongo Beti, "L'enfant noir de Camara Laye," *Présence Africaine* 16 (1953): 420.

33. Sembène, *Archives sonores.*

4. Colonial Violence

1. One should not infer from this "honorary title" that Aliin Sitooye Jaata ruled over a kingdom. Far from it, Kabrousse (also spelled Cabrousse) is only a small settlement, a coastal village just a couple of miles away from the seaside resort of Cap Skirring. But since Jaata's days, a revolutionary aura hangs over the area, and to this day it is used as a home base by MFDC secessionists.

2. God of thunder in Joola cosmogony.

3. *Afrique Occidentale Française* (French West Africa).

4. *Afrique Equatoriale Française* (French Equatorial Africa).

5. Statements made by Abbé Diamacoune Senghor during an interview with the author, Ziguinchor, 1997.

6. Ibid.

7. Sembène, *Archives sonores*.

5. The Lebu Ghettos of Dakar Plateau

1. Mongo Beti, *Ville cruelle* (Paris: Présence Africaine, 1971) (published under the pen name Eza Boto). In this novel the Cameroonian writer describes the city of Tanga so vividly, with its Manichean division into two areas, the (European) North and the (native) South, that it has been ever since regarded as *the* prototype of a highly segregated colonial city.

2. We speak here of "reservations" inasmuch as after the arrival of Pinet Laprade and his flotilla on May 11, 1857, the Lebus were gradually deprived of their lands. The first cadastral plan was drafted in 1858 and eventually would be amended and expanded with two alignment plans in 1862 and 1876. From 1903 to 1908, governor general Ernest Roume implemented an urban planning policy in which the Lebus would be left with only a small tract of land surrounded, like a small island in the middle of the ocean, by French residences and trade establishments.

3. Initiation rites for the circumcised conducted by their guide into adult life, the *selbé*.

4. The initiation consists of songs, riddles, etc. The point is to teach them how to live in the "Sanctuary of Man."

5. A profane, erotic and very provocative dance that was highly popular in urban areas around the '30s.

6. Maurice Fall, interview with the author, Guédiawaye, Dakar, 1996.

7. Maurice Fall remained one of Sembène's closest friends until his death in 1997. He worked at the Land Registry office. He befriended Sembène during the '30s.

8. Françoise Pfaff, *The Cinema of Ousmane Sembène, a Pioneer of African Film* (Westport, Conn.: Greenwood Press, 1984).

9. Ousmane Sembène, *Mandabi* (The money order), feature film, 90 min., Filmii Doomireew, 1968.

10. Maurice Fall, interview with the author, 1996.

11. Ibid.

12. Laye, *Dark Child*. See especially the chapter devoted to the circumcision rite.

13. Boubacar Boris Diop, interview with the author, 1996. Today one of Senegal's finest and most prominent writers, Diop was heavily influenced by Ousmane Sembène in the '60s.

14. A kind of poem in movement whereby the wrestling champion dances to the rhythm of drums and in which he brags about his skills, taunts his opponents, and entertains the spectators.

15. *L'appel des arènes,* a novel by Senegalese novelist Aminata Sow Fall (Dakar: NEA, 1982). It is the story of a young schoolboy who ditches classes and gradually drifts, away from school, toward the fascinating world of traditional wrestling where frantic tom-tom beats urge wrestlers to step into the arena.

16. T.N.: The *fanal* is a festival during which young urbanites from the Four Communes (Dakar, Saint-Louis, Gorée, and Rufisque) display their dancing and singing skills, and the unique aspects of their cultural riches and diversity as well.

17. Doudou Guèye, interview with the author, 1997.

18. Ibid.

19. Mokhtar Diop is one of Sembène's childhood friends who kept close ties with him. To give one example of this enduring friendship: Sembène's last born was named after Mokhtar Diop. The two friends used to meet every Sunday afternoon at Gallè Ceddo.

20. Ousmane Sembène, observation made in 1990 in an African Literature class at Smith College, Northampton, Massachusetts.

21. Maurice Jacquin was a prominent French film producer. He died in 1975.

22. Sembène, *O pays,* p. 63.

6. The World of Labor

1. Djib Diédhiou, "An Interview with Ousmane Sembène," *Le Soleil,* November 7, 1993, pp. 8–9.

2. Sembène, *O pays,* p. 58.

3. The nickname "Rafet" means "handsome man." It would later inspire Sembène, during the writing of *God's Bits of Wood,* to name one of his characters "Daouda Beau-Gosse" (Daouda the handsome boy).

4. Abdoulaye Wade, born on May 29, 1926, in Saint-Louis, is the current president of Senegal. After years of fighting in the opposition, Wade, who was trained as an economist and a lawyer, was voted into office as the third president of Senegal on March 19, 2000. He was re-elected in 2007 for a second term—reduced to 5 years in the Constitution of the second republic.

5. A Wolof word referring to an individual who specializes in the collection and recycling of miscellaneous objects for the purpose of putting them on sale and thus back into the circulation of goods. The *baay jagal* goes from house to house and from market to market to respectively collect and sell these used objects.

6. Ousmane Sembène, informal talk with the author.

7. The Experience of Racism

1. Assane Sylla, *Le peuple lébou de la presqu'île du Cap-Vert* (Dakar: NEA, 1992).

2. For more on the political structures in place before colonization, as well as some detailed descriptions of daily life in the various kingdoms of Senegal, see Cheikh Anta Diop, *Precolonial Black Africa: A Comparative Study of the Political*

and *Social Systems of Europe and Black Africa, from Antiquity to the Formation of Modern States,* trans. Harold J. Salemson (Chicago: Lawrence Hill Books, 1987).

3. Cheikh Hamidou Kane, *Les gardiens du temple* (Paris: Stock, 1995).

4. Abdoulaye Sadji, *Tounka* (Paris: Présence Africaine, 1965).

5. Ibid.

6. Cheikh Hamidou Kane, *L'aventure ambiguë* (Paris: Julliard, 1961). Kane's novel describes the gradual intrusion of the French colonial system into the *Fuuta* (northern Senegal) and the resulting political decline of the aristocracy in that region.

7. Sylla, *Le peuple,* p. 53.

8. Bara Diouf, "L'itinéraire d'un enfant du siècle," *Le Soleil,* November 7, 1993, p. 11.

9. Ibid., p. 12.

10. Ousmane Sembène, *Camp de Thiaroye,* long feature, 1988. This movie chronicles the bloody repression, on November 1, 1944, of African colonial soldiers protesting against unfair treatments based on racism, notably their lower pay in comparison to what their French "comrades" received; but the movie also addresses the larger and painful issue of colonial massacres that were perpetrated not only in Senegal, but also in Algeria, Madagascar, Ivory Coast, Congo-Brazzaville, and Indochina.

11. Quoted in Cheikh Faty Faye, *L'opinion publique dakaroise, 1940–1944* (Master's thesis, University of Dakar, 1973).

12. Second largest religious brotherhood in Senegal, after the *Murids.*

13. Faye, *L'opinion,* p. 25.

14. This bleak period of shortage and starvation is evoked in the film *Camp de Thiaroye.*

15. Faye, *L'opinion,* p. 62.

16. Ibid., p. 64.

17. Ousmane Sembène, informal talk with the author.

18. On the actual events on which *Camp de Thiaroye* is based, see Mbaye Guèye, "Le 1ᵉʳ décembre 1944 à Thiaroye, ou le massacre de tirailleurs sénégalais, anciens prisonniers de guerre," *Revue sénégalaise d'histoire* 1 (1995).

19. Diouf, "L'itinéraire," p. 12.

20. Lamine Guèye (1891–1968), who had close ties with Léon Blum and the French socialists, founded in 1930 the first Senegalese chapter of the SFIO. In 1945 he was Senegal's representative in the French National Assembly. But Guèye's most enduring legacy is the 1946 bill, called the Lamine Guèye Bill, which granted French citizenship to all persons from the Overseas Territories.

21. Vieyra, *Ousmane Sembène, cineaste.*

22. Sylla, *Le peuple,* p. 60.

23. For more on the *Layènes* and religious brotherhoods in Senegal, see especially Khadim Mbacké, *Sufism and Religious Brotherhoods in Senegal,* translated from the French by Eric Ross and edited by John Hunwick (Princeton, N.J.: Markus Wiener, 2005).

24. Sylla, *Le people.*

25. The Rebeuss Correctional Facility is located right behind the Bloc des Madeleines, the District Court.

26. Doudou Guèye, interview with the author, Dakar, 1996.

8. "Here We Come, Marshal!"

1. A reference to the famous Sonnet IX, "France, mère des arts," in Joachim Du Bellay's *Regrets* (1558).

2. Faye, *L'opinion;* Guèye, "Le 1er décembre 1944 à Thiaroye."

3. Doudou Guèye, interview with the author, 1996.

4. Kane, *L'aventure ambiguë.*

5. Maurice Fall, interview with the author, 1997.

6. Issa Sembène, interview with the author, Rufisque, 1996.

7. Moore, *Evolution of an African Artist.*

8. It must be noted that there were military bases not only in Senegal, but in other colonial territories as well. There were Camp Marchand in Rufisque for the 5th Colonial Infantry Regiment and another base in Kati, in French Sudan; there was also the Third Transportation Company in Niamey, Niger.

9. Ousmane Sembène, *Black Docker,* trans. Ros Schwartz (London: Heinemann, 1986), p. 1.

10. Sembène, *O pays,* p. 59.

11. Djibril Mbengue, interview with the author, Rufisque, 1996.

12. Antoine de Saint-Exupéry, *Wind, Sand, and Stars,* translated from the French by Lewis Galantière and illustrated by John O'H. Cosgrave II (New York: Harcourt Brace and World, 1940), p. 227.

13. Sembène, *O pays,* pp. 116–17.

9. The Winds of Change

The epigraph is from Sembène, *Black Docker,* pp. 1–2.

1. Maurice Fall, interview with the author, 1997.

2. Comment made during the interview given to Houston Public Television.

3. Léopold Sédar Senghor, "Tyaroye," in *The Collected Poetry,* trans. Melvin Dixon (Charlottesville: University Press of Virginia, 1991), p. 68.

4. Ousmane Sembène, comment made after the screening of *Camp de Thiaroye* at Rice University, Houston, Texas, 1996.

5. Xavier Yacono, *Les étapes de la décolonisation française* (Paris: PUF, 1971), p. 58.

6. Charles de Gaulle, "Inaugural Address at the Brazzaville Conference," quoted in ibid.

7. Guèye, "Le 1er décembre 1944 à Thiaroye," p. 18.

8. Sylla, *Le peuple lébou,* p. 74.

9. Ousmane Sembène, "Un amour de la rue sablonneuse," a short story in *Voltaïque* (Paris: Présence Africaine, 1962), p. 16.

10. Sembène, *O pays,* p. 164.

11. Ousmane Sembène, *Xala,* feature film, 90 min., 1973.

12. Sounkaré is a key figure in *God's Bits of Wood* (1960). An old watchman in the train station's depot in Thiès, he has always managed to stay away from labor movements. After an accident at work, he is seriously incapacitated and has to spend the remaining years of his life in prayers and meditation. During the strike, left entirely alone and, like all the strikers, suffering hunger, he wavers in his beliefs and then launches into a passionate, Job-like questioning of the divine and the value of faith. Later on, he will die from starvation and be eaten by two rats.

13. Ousmane Sembène, *God's Bits of Wood* trans. Francis Price (New York: Doubleday, 1962), p. 179.

14. Ibid., p. 180.

15. Ousmane Sembène, interview with Carrie Moore, Paris, 1971.

16. Sembène, *God's Bits of Wood,* trans. Price, p. 319.

17. Sembène, *Black Docker,* p. 116.

10. The Moment of Truth

1. Yacono, *Les étapes,* p. 59.

2. Ibid., p. 62.

3. For more on Senegal's long, tortuous, and vibrant political history, including the colonial legacy of collusion between political authorities and religious leaders, see, inter alia, Jacques Mariel Nzouankeu, *Les partis politiques sénégalais* (Dakar: Clairafrique, 1984); Christian Roche, *Le Sénégal à la conquête de son indépendance, 1939–1960: Chronique de la vie politique et syndicale, de l'Empire français à l'Indépendance* (Paris: Karthala, 2001); Assane Seck, *Sénégal: Emergence d'une démocratie moderne (1945–2005): Un itinéraire politique,* preface by Djibril Samb (Paris: Karthala, 2005); L. C. Behrman, *Muslim Brotherhoods and Politics in Senegal* (Cambridge, Mass.: Harvard University Press, 1970).

4. Ousmane Sembène, informal talk with the author.

5. Sembène, *Camp de Thiaroye.*

6. Diouf, "L'itinéraire," p. 8.

7. Ibid.

8. Ferdinand Oyono, *Une vie de boy* (Paris: Julliard, 1960).

9. Sembène, *God's Bits of Wood,* trans. Price, p. 52.

10. For some good background information on the history of labor movements in Senegal, see Iba Der Thiam, *L'évolution politique et syndicale du Sénégal colonial de 1840 à 1936* (Paris: Université de Paris I, 1983), 9 vol. (Postdoctoral thesis).

11. See the "Author's Note" to *God's Bits of Wood.*

12. The famous "long walk" from Thiès to Dakar organized by women in 1947 bears testimony to female agency and resilience during the railroad workers' strike. See the chapter devoted to the episode, "From Thiès to Dakar: The March of the Women," in *God's Bits of Wood,* trans. Price, pp. 253–277.

13. Ibid., pp. 53–54.

14. The anecdote was revealed in 1998 by Codou Diop, Ibrahima Sarr's widow. See the volume published by the Confederation of Senegalese Workers (CNTS) on

the occasion of the 50th anniversary of the railroad workers' strike, held in Thiès, October 11–12, 1998.

15. Sembène, *God's Bits of Wood*, trans. Price, p. 206.

16. Maurice Fall, interview with the author, 1997.

17. See Senghor, *The Collected Poetry*, p. 149.

18. Maurice Fall, interview with the author, 1997.

19. Ousmane Sembène, informal talk with the author, Dakar, 1997.

20. Sembène, *Black Docker*, p. 49.

21. Ibid., p. 117.

22. Ousmane Sembène, "La noire de . . . ," in *Voltaïque*, p. 74. As already mentioned, the short story eventually would be made into the movie *Black Girl*.

23. Frantz Fanon, *Black Skin, White Masks*, trans. Charles L. Markmann (New York: Grove Press, 1967), p. 23.

24. Maurice Fall, interview with the author, 1997.

25. Sembène, "La noire de . . . ," in *Voltaïque*, p. 174.

11. "The Village"

1. Michel Richard, "Introduction," *Le Point,* April 23, 1999.

2. Ibid.

3. Laurent Theis, *Le Point,* April 23, 1999, p. 93.

4. Sembène, *Archives sonores.*

5. Theis, *Le Point,* p. 96.

6. Ancient Greek name of Marseilles.

7. Legend mentioned by Richard in his introduction to the special issue of *Le Point,* April 23, 1999.

8. A *pied-noir* (literally, "black foot") is a Frenchman born in colonial North Africa (Tunisia, Morocco and, mostly, Algeria).

9. Jean-Louis Parisis, *Des Navires et des hommes: deux siècles de navigation en Méditerranée et au-delà* (Aix-en-Provence: Edisud, 2000), p. 32.

10. Quoted in Parisis, *Des Navires et des hommes,* p. 41.

11. Ibid., p. 72.

12. A *gobi* is an army recruit enrolled as a private second class and who, in the course of his military service, has not earned a single stripe.

13. Roger Duchêne and Jean Contrucci, *Marseille: 2600 ans d'histoire* (Paris: Fayard, 2002).

14. Term used to designate Moroccan soldiers who served in auxiliary units attached to the French army between 1908 and 1956. Quoted in Duchêne and Contrucci, *Marseille,* p. 674.

15. Sembène, *Archives sonores.*

16. Paul Belsanti, retired docker and a CGT member. In 1998, I interviewed him at the headquarters of the Association of Retired Dockers (CGT-affiliated) in Marseilles, at the Quai de la Joliette.

17. Sembène, *Black Docker,* p. 41.

18. Ibid., p. 59.

19. Ibid., p. 62.

20. Ibid., p. 63.

21. Ibid., p. 41.

22. Ibid.

23. Brigitte Bertoncello and Sylvie Bredeloup, "A la recherche du docker noir," in *Dockers de la Méditerranée à la Mer du Nord: des quais et des hommes dans l'histoire,* ed. Telemme Research Group (Aix-en-Provence: Edisud, 1999).

24. According to Bertoncello and Bredeloup, ibid., p. 139. Unfortunately, the authors do not provide further details on the matter.

25. See Claude McKay, *Banjo: A Story without a Plot* (New York: Harvest Book, 1929).

26. Sembène, *Black Docker,* p. 41.

27. Another term used to designate the Mandingos.

28. Small ethnic group, originally from Bissau Guinea, also found in Casamance.

29. Sembène, *Black Docker,* p. 42.

30. Philippe Dewitte, *Les mouvements nègres en France: 1919–1939* (Paris: L'Harmattan, 1985), p. 279.

31. T.N.: "Bouki" is the name of the dull-witted and cowardly hyena in Senegalese folktales that is always outsmarted by Leuk-the-hare, the trickster figure. See Birago Diop, *Les Contes d'Amadou Koumba* (Paris: Fasquelle, 1947). Translated by Dorothy S. Blair as *Tales of Amadou Koumba* (Oxford: Oxford University Press, 1966).

32. Sembène, *Black Docker,* pp. 56–57.

33. Ibrahima Barro, interview with the author. According to Barro, who worked as lighting engineer in more than half of Sembène's movies, it was the latter who convinced him of the absolute necessity of coming back to work in Senegal.

34. Sembène, *Black Docker,* p. 48.

35. Ibid., pp. 64–65.

36. Dewitte, *Les mouvements nègres,* p. 79.

37. Sembène, *Black Docker,* p. 58.

38. Ousmane Sembène, "Lettres de France," *Voltaïque,* p. 76.

39. Ousmane Sembène, *Black Docker,* p. 74.

40. Ibid.

41. Albert Cervoni, "Ousmane Sembène, docker et romancier," *La Marseillaise,* October 1956, p. 10.

12. The Docker

1. Alfred Pacini and Dominique Pons, *Docker à Marseille* (Paris: Payot, 1996), p. 54.

2. Sembène, *Archives sonores.*

3. French term used for Eastern Timor during the colonial period.

4. Pacini and Pons, *Docker à Marseille.*

5. Albert Londres, "*Marseille, porte du sud,*" in *Œuvres Complètes,* presented by Pierre Assouline (Paris: Arléa, 2007), p. 349.

6. Literally, wharf dogs.

7. Londres, *"Marseille, porte du sud."*

8. Alfred Pacini, son of Italian immigrants, was very active in the *Front Populaire* (Popular Front). In the early 1950s he was elected member of the Marseilles city council.

9. Sembène, "Chaïba," in *Voltaïque*, p. 124.

10. Pacini and Dupons, *Docker à Marseille*, p. 134.

11. Ibid., p. 64.

12. See Emile Belsenti, interview with the author at the headquarters of the Union of Dockers (CGT chapter), Place de la Joliette, Marseilles, 1997.

13. T.N.: The French term *portefaix* also designated the docker in the second half of the nineteenth century. *Portefaix* literally means "carrier of burden," but it can also take the stronger meaning of "beast of burden," which is obviously less euphemistic and speaks more to Sembène's situation as described here.

14. Sembène, *Black Docker*, p. 77.

15. See Elisabeth Claverie, "De l'artisanat à l'ère industrielle sur les quais de Marseille: du portefaix au docker (XIXe–XXe siècles)," in *Dockers de la Méditerranée à la mer du Nord*, p. 80.

16. Londres, *"Marseille, porte du sud,"* pp. 349–350.

17. Sembène, *Black Docker*, pp. 69–70.

18. Ibid., p. 71.

19. *Acconiers* in French, meaning those who are supposed to manage the freight goods stored in the harbor's warehouses by the dockers, whom they hire for this task.

20. Quoted in Pacini and Dupons, *Docker à Marseille*, pp. 120–121.

21. Michel Libermann and Sembène were active in CGT and other leftist organizations or intellectual movements in Marseilles during the '50s. Libermann joined the French *Résistance* in 1944, when he was only 14.

22. Patrick Chamoiseau, *L'Esclave vieil homme et le molosse* (Paris: Gallimard, 1997).

23. Sembène, *Black Docker*, p. 74.

24. Ibid., pp. 82–83.

25. Odette Arouh, friend and confidante of Sembène's, was a member of PCF and MRAP, in whose circles they both met.

26. Simone Schwartz-Bart, *Pluie et vent sur Telumée miracle* (Paris: Seuil, 1972).

27. Odette Arouh, interview with the author, Marseilles, 1996.

28. Bernard Worms, interview with the author, Marseilles, 1996. Like Odette Arouh and Michel Libermann, Bernard Worms is a Marseilles Jew who was actively involved in the *Résistance* during the war and the German occupation.

13. The Militant

1. Emile Belsenti, interview with the author at the Union of Dockers, Place de la Joliette, Marseilles, 1997.

2. Sembène, *Archives sonores*.

3. Testimony of Marius Colombini, a former *pointeur* (supervisor) at the *Messageries Maritimes*; secretary-general of the Union of Supervisors; secretary-general of the *Union départementale des syndicats* (Local Confederation of Labor); secretary of the PCF Federation; and elected member of the PC's central committee. Quoted in Pacini and Pons, *Docker à Marseille,* p. 300.

4. Marius Colombini, quoted in ibid., p. 303.

5. Pacini and Pons, *Docker à Marseille,* p. 70.

6. Ousmane Sembène, interview with Moore, *Evolution of an African Artist.*

7. Ibid.

8. George Padmore, quoted in Dewitte, *Les mouvements nègres,* pp. 285–286.

9. Ibid.

10. Ousmane Sembène, interview with Moore, *Evolution of an African Artist.*

11. Ibid.

12. Ibid.

13. Ibid.

14. Bernard Worms, interview with the author, Marseilles, 1997.

15. Moore, *Evolution of an African Artist.*

16. Sembène, *Black Docker,* p. 119.

17. See interview with Moore, *Evolution of an African Artist.*

18. Bernard Worms, interview with the author, Marseilles, 1997.

19. Ibid.

20. Michel Libermann, interview with the author, 1998.

21. Interview with a group of retired CGT dockers, La Joliette, Marseilles, 1997.

22. CGT militants.

23. Bernard Worms, interview with the author, Marseilles, 1997.

24. In the correspondence I entertained with him over the years, Sembène ritually ended his faxes and letters with the formula: "The struggle continues!" thus underwriting one of his favorite witty remarks: "The old guard dies but does not surrender."

25. Saint-Exupéry, *Terre des hommes,* p. 160; trans. Galantière. T.N.: Strangely enough, the passage quoted here has been omitted in this English translation.

26. In the parlance of French labor organizations, this color always connotes deceit, betrayal, and cowardice.

27. Bernard Worms, interview with the author, Marseilles, 1997.

28. Tunisia also co-produced *Camp de Thiaroye* (1984) and *Faat Kiné* (2000). *Moolaade* (2004) was edited in Morocco. The Algerian drama, it should be noted, features prominently in Sembène's early literary works, including *Black Docker* and *Voltaïque.*

29. Note also that Sembène often uses his art to signal a critical, but not judgmental, attitude toward his former companions, who have become, in his view, mercenaries turning their weapons against themselves.

30. T.N.: Sembène uses the Wolof expression *bokk mbar,* which means, literally, hut-mate, and refers to companions with whom one shared the "sanctuary of man" during the period of circumcision. It could be rendered as "blood brother" to indi-

cate, as Sembène certainly does, that a lifelong pact of blood is also sealed between the circumcised.

31. Ousmane Sembène, *The Money Order, with White Genesis,* trans. Clive Wake (London: Heinemann, 1972), p. 2. Emphasis in original.

32. In 1894, Alfred Dreyfus, a Jewish captain in the French army, was wrongly accused of spying for Germany. After a sham trial, he was convicted and deported to Ile du Diable (Devil's Island). The affair is known to have divided French society, notably its intelligentsia—which actually emerged out of it as a self-conscious social and historical force. It was in this context that the novelist Emile Zola famously wrote his scathing open letter to President Félix Faure, "J'accuse," published in *L'Aurore* on January 13, 1898.

33. Willie McGee, executed for alleged rape in 1951, in Mississippi.

34. Odette Arouh, interview with the author, Marseilles, 1998.

35. Bernard Worms, interview with the author, Marseilles, 1998.

36. Michel Libermann, interview with the author, Marseilles, 1998.

37. Ibid.

38. Bernard Worms, interview with the author, Marseilles, 1996.

39. Ousmane Sembène, "Liberté," *Action Poétique* (*Les peuples opprimés*), 5, no. 2 (1956): 29–32.

40. Sembène, *Archives sonores.*

41. Pierre Haffner, "Eléments pour un autoportrait magnétique: Ousmane Sembène," *CinemAction,* ed. Guy Hennebelle, September 1985.

42. Ibid., p. 23.

43. Ibid., p. 21.

44. Ibid.

45. Ibid., p. 22.

46. Ibid., p. 21.

47. Sembène, *Voltaïque.*

48. Ibid., p. 117.

49. Ibid., p. 121.

50. Sembène, "Liberté."

51. "The only way out: total independence. The only means thereto: a mass-based anti-imperialist movement."

52. The harbor in Bissau, capital city of Bissau-Guinea.

14. The Fire-Giver

1. T.N.: Sembène tersely uses the French word *enferme* to refer both to the viewers sitting in a movie theater and to the limits this situation sets to their imagination. It is a doubly passive situation, and the word "captive" seems closest to conveying this subtle ambivalence, in the sense that they are also *captivated.*

2. Ousmane Sembène, interview given to Houston Public Television, Texas, 1996.

3. Sembène, *Voltaïque,* p. 7.

4. Haffner, "Eléments pour un autoportrait magnétique," p. 21.

5. Jean-Michel Guiraud, *La vie intellectuelle et artistique à Marseille à l'époque de Vichy et sous l'occupation (1940–1944)*, brocade edition (Paris: J. Laffitte, 1999), p. 383.

6. Haffner, "Eléments pour un autoportrait magnétique," p. 20.

7. Ibid., p. 21.

8. T.N.: *taaxuraan* is a type of oral poetry performance, accompanied with the tama, a percussion instrument. It originated from the Sine Saloum area, the native region of Sembène's grandmother, Diodio Sène. The poems *taaxuraan* singers compose are always didactic and moralizing. They are mostly sung during rites of passage—during seasonal rites such as rain dances or ceremonial rites such as circumcision and marriages.

9. Haffner, p. 21.

10. It will be remembered that DuBois visited Russia in 1927 and subsequently became a member of the Communist Party.

11. Sembène, *Black Docker,* p. 73.

12. Ibid.

13. Colloquial term for a docker in Marseilles.

14. Ibid., p. 45.

15. Moore, *Evolution of an African Artist.*

16. Jacqueline Tavernier-Courbin, *The Call of the Wild: A Naturalistic Romance* (New York: Twayne, 1994), p. 3.

17. Jack London, *Martin Eden* (New York: Macmillan, 1909).

18. Jack London, *The People of the Abyss* (New York: Macmillan, 1903). In this novel, London takes the reader on a journey to the underworld of working-class neighborhoods in late nineteenth-century London.

19. Moore, *Evolution of an African Artist.*

20. Jack London, *The Road* (electronic resource) (New Brunswick, N.J.: Rutgers University Press, 2006), p. 22.

21. Moore, *Evolution of an African Artist.*

22. Ibid.

23. Informal talk with the author, Rabat, April 2004.

24. Ibid.

25. Moore, *Evolution of an African Artist.*

26. Sembène, *Black Docker,* p. 84.

27. Moore, *Evolution of an African Artist.*

28. Ibid., p. 224.

29. Word of Berber origins, meaning "inner desert," areas deep inside an arid region. Nowadays, in a more colloquial sense, it designates any faraway place set in the middle of nowhere.

30. Sembène, "Liberté."

31. Moore, *Evolution of an African Artist.*

32. Liliane Kesteloot provides some good biographical sketches of all these writers in her classical anthology. See Liliane Kesteloot, *Anthologie négro-africaine: La littérature de 1918 à 1981* (Paris: Marabout, 1987).

33. Moore, *Evolution of an African Artist.*

34. Haffner, "Eléments pour un autoportrait magnétique," p. 24.

35. Moore, *Evolution of an African Artist.*

36. Ibid.

37. Short for Aix-en-Provence.

38. Ibid.

39. Haffner, "Eléments pour un autoportrait magnétique," p. 22.

40. Moore, *Evolution of an African Artist.*

41. Ibid.

42. Haffner, "Eléments pour un autoportrait magnétique," pp. 23–24.

43. Moore, *Evolution of an African Artist.*

44. Odette Arouh claims that the novel had been for "years in the making," but this statement is hard, if not impossible, to corroborate.

45. Bernard Worms, interview with the author, 1996.

46. Sembène, "Liberté."

47. Cervoni, "Ousmane Sembène, docker et romancier," p. 6.

48. Ibid., p. 7.

49. Jacques Roumain, *Masters of the Dew,* trans. Langston Hughes and Mercer Cook (New York: Reynal & Hitchcock, 1947).

50. Sembène, "Liberté."

51. Mark Donskoi (1901–1981), Soviet film director known for his three-part cinematic biography of Maxim Gorky, the *Gorky Trilogy.*

Conclusion

1. For instance, seven of Sembène's novels have been translated into English, including *Black Docker, God's Bits of Wood,* and *The Last of the Empire.*

INDEX

Samba Gadjigo is Professor of French and former Head of the French Department at Mount Holyoke College. He is author of *Ecole blanche, Afrique noire: L'image de l'ecole coloniale dans le roman africaine francophone* and editor of *Ousmane Sembène: Dialogue with Critics and Writers.*